S A

977.01   Up country: voices from
UP   the midwestern wilderness

DATE DUE

29970

STOCKTON
Township Public Library
Stockton, IL

Up Country

Voices from the Midwestern Wilderness

Compiled and Edited
by William Joseph Seno

Round River Publishing Company • Madison

© Copyright, 1985, by William Joseph Seno
Published by Round River Publishing Co.
        P. O. Box 3324
        Madison, WI 53704

Book design by Sally Owen Orth
Typesetting by Impressions, Inc.
Printing and binding by American Printing Co.

The following have generously permitted the use of art that appears in *Up Country* on the pages indicated:

National Museum of American Art (formerly National Collection by Fine Arts), Smithsonian Institution. Gift of Mrs. Joseph Harrison, Jr. Pages 51, 76, 84, 118, 131, 182, 183, 219, 229, 237, and back cover.

State Historical Society of Wisconsin. Pages 5, 22, 33, 67, 88, 112, 146, 158, 198, 204, 210, 212, and front cover.

Illinois Bell Telephone Company. Pages 56 and 232.

Michigan Bell Telephone Company. 444 Michigan Ave., Detroit, MI 48226. Pages 40 and 174.

Irvin Hanson of Spicer, Minnesota. Pages 14 and 60.

ISBN 0-933437-00-5
Library of Congress Catalog Card Number 85-60995

CONTENTS

TO THE READER

Over 300 years ago a broken board was found deep in the North American wilderness. On it were scrawled the words *NOUS SOMMES TOUS SAUVAGES*—"We are all savages." The board was the remnant of an expedition launched in 1679 by Frenchmen who dreamed of founding an empire to extend across the heart of the continent. The French fell victim to shipwreck, hunger, desertion and Indian attack. Finally, they offered this cryptic surrender to the all-encompassing wilderness: "We are all savages."

Other Frenchmen entered the wilderness with other dreams: fur traders with dreams of fortune, soldiers with dreams of conquest, missionaries with dreams of converting the Indians to Christianity. All encountered hardships and dangers in a wild region they knew as the Upper Country.

Today we know this region as the Midwest.

Up Country is a compilation of journals, letters and memoirs written by early adventurers in the Midwest. The book opens in 1656 with conjecture about the unseen wilderness, and closes with the surrender of Chief Black Hawk in 1832. *Up Country* is a book of firsthand experience, offering impressions of primeval landscapes and of initial contacts between Europeans and Native Americans. Unfortunately, the editor found no early writings by Native Americans, so this book is unavoidably prejudiced against the natives.

Many passages from the original writings were rephrased in *Up Country* for easier comprehension; yet this book remains true to the content and spirit of the original narratives. Sources for all chapters are cited in a bibliography.

Up Country is illustrated with paintings and drawings by some of America's best frontier artists, among them George Catlin, Frederic Remington and Seth Eastman.

It is hoped the reader will approach *Up Country* with the spirit of an armchair explorer discovering a new world.

W. J. S.
March 1, 1985

A COUNTRY FULL OF DARKNESS

Jean de Quens   1656

In the year 1656, the young colony of New France was comprised of but a few frontier settlements along Canada's St. Lawrence River. There the French were besieged by a fierce and powerful Indian confederacy—the Five Nations of the Iroquois. "They come like foxes, attack like lions, and depart like birds," wrote one Frenchman of the Iroquois. But not all Indians were enemies to the French. Friendly natives sometimes arrived at Montreal, after long canoe voyages from their homelands far to the west. On such occasions, the French eagerly traded for valuable furs, and asked about the western wilderness—a mysterious land the French called the "Upper Country."

About the end of August there appeared 250 Ottawa savages in 50 canoes, loaded with the treasures of their country. They came to traffic with the French and to ask that some of the priests of our company be sent to instruct them in the thick forests of their country, distant 1,200 miles from Quebec. We responded in their fashion by giving presents. All they demanded was willingly accorded.

We have learned that toward the north there are numerous lakes that would readily pass for freshwater seas. The great Lake of the Hurons and another nearby are equal in size to the Caspian Sea.

1

Our attention has been directed toward a number of nations in the neighborhood of the "Nation of the Sea" [Winnebagoes]. The Liniouek [Illinois], their neighbors, number about 60 villages; the Nadouesiouack [Sioux] number all of 40; the Ponarak [Chippewa] at least 30; the Kiristinons [Cree] surpass all these in numbers, as their country extends as far as the North Sea [Hudson Bay]. All of these people make war upon other more distant nations. So it is true that men act as wolves toward their fellow men, and that the number of the mad is infinite. These madmen destroy themselves in contending who shall give the law to the others.

While the Ottawas were engaged in making their little trades, 30 young Frenchmen equipped themselves to accompany the Ottawas to their country, and to bring back furs. I gave the Ottawas, as guides on their path to salvation, Father Leonard Garreau and Father Gabriel Dreuillettes, aged evangelical workers, well versed in the Huron and Algonquin languages. The fathers rejoiced to be the first chosen to carry the name of Jesus Christ into a country full of tribulation, darkness and death.

> *The expedition never reached the Upper Country. De Quens later wrote, "The Lower Iroquois, who have never been willing to live at peace with our allies, in an instant cut the thread of our hope. They attacked those poor people, and killed one of the fathers."*

2

CAESARS IN THE WILDERNESS

Pierre Esprit Radisson   1658

Two bold soldiers of fortune embarked from Montreal in 1658 to explore the Upper Country. Pierre Esprit Radisson and his brother-in-law, Medard Chouart de Groseilliers, were renegade fur traders, seasoned by past hardships in the wilderness. They knew their canoe route up the Ottawa River toward Lake Huron would be guarded by fierce Iroquois war parties.

We propose to the Governor of Quebec that we venture our lives to explore the most remote countries. The governor gives us leave only if we will carry two of his servants along with us and give them a share of the profit. My brother is vexed at such a demand, to take inexperienced men to their ruin. He is vexed that the governor would compare two of his servants with us, who have ventured our lives for so many years. Nor is there anyone who has the courage to undertake what we have done.

We make the governor a slight answer. We tell him that, for our part, we know that we are discoverers rather than governors. We tell him that we are our own masters and servants. The governor is much displeased at this, and commands us not to go without his leave.

The month of August brings a company of wildmen to Montreal, who have taken incredible pains to come from the Upper Country.

3

They arrive in seven canoes. We make gifts to these wildmen, who wish with all their hearts that we return with them. We tell them that the governor has a mind to send servants with them instead, and to forbid us to go. The wildmen say they will not accept servants into their company, but tell us they will wait for us two days at a prairie 15 miles from Trois Rivieres.

We do not let them wait so long. That very night we embark at midnight, my brother having the keys to the borough. As we pass opposite the fort, the sentry calls out, "Who goes there?" My brother gives his name. The sentry answers, "God give you a good voyage."

We go on the rest of the night, and the next day we find the wildmen at the River of the Meadows [now Ottawa River of Ontario Province]. This river is much divided into very swift streams. The Iroquois enemy is to be feared here, which makes us pull our canoes through the torrents. We suffer much. After three days we see the tracks of seven canoes and fires yet burning. We know the people are not enemies, but imagine they are Octanaks [Ottawas] going up country. We take no rest until we overtake them. We join them, and are 14 canoes together, all going to the Upper Lake [Lake Superior].

Yet the danger has scarcely begun, for the Iroquois enemy has fortified himself along this river, and he goes up and down it to make new slaughters.

Two days later we reach a portage and send one man ahead to make the kettle boil, for we have just killed two deer. He goes scarcely half way when he meets an Iroquois warrior. I think both are much surprised. The Iroquois has a bundle of beaver pelts that he leaves behind without much ado. Our wildman does the same, and runs to warn us. Out of breath, he gasps "Nadonnee." We run to the height of the carrying place, as our wildmen take up their weapons with all speed. On the way we find the bundle of beaver pelts the enemy left, showing us that they too are in a fright. We gain the water side where we see the enemies landing two canoes and charging their guns to set upon us. We prevent this by shooting at them, and they forsake the place.

4

Fur trader, by Frederic Remington

Their number is not enough to resist ours, so they retire into their fort and summon the rest of their men, in hopes to save it. In this they are far mistaken, for we make a furious assault, not sparing time to make shields, but using only beaver pelts tied together. The Iroquois spare not their gun powder, but make more noise than hurt.

5

Darkness covers the earth, which favors us.

To overcome them the sooner, we fill a barrel full of gun powder, attach a fuse, and tie the barrel to the end of a long pole near the foot of the fort. I warn the wildmen that as soon as the barrel explodes, they must enter with hatchet and sword in hand and break down the fort. We execute our plan. The barrel explodes. The enemy has never seen the like. They sing, expecting death, or take to their heels at the smoke and noise our machine makes, slaughtering many. Seeing themselves so betrayed, they let us rush into their fort. We are mingled pell mell, so that we cannot recognize one another in that skirmish of blows. Now there comes a terrible storm and rain, with such noise to terrify the strongest men. In that darkness, everyone looks for shelter, not thinking of pursuing the warriors who lie half dead. To my thinking, this is something extraordinary. I believe the devil himself made this storm, to allow the Iroquois to escape from our hands, so they may destroy more innocents another time.

As the storm passes, we come together. I am convinced that some of our wildmen think themselves captured, although they are at liberty. Some sing their death songs, although they have no wounds. Those with confidence assure the others of the victory—the enemy has been routed.

We make a great fire and hastily build up the fort again. We visit the dead and wounded, and search for those missing. We find 11 enemy slain and only two of ours, besides seven wounded. We tend to the wounds of our companions, who show their courage by singing louder than those who are well. We burn our dead comrades, it being the custom to reduce to ashes those slain in battle. It is an honor to give them such a burial.

Some wildmen are busy tying four captives who did not escape. Many wildmen fill their bellies with the flesh of dead enemies. We boil some of it, and fill kettles with the rest. The greatest mark of our victory is that we have ten heads and four prisoners, whom we hope to take to the Upper Country, there to burn them at our leisure. The wildmen plague the unfortunate prisoners, plucking out their nails one by one.

The next morning, after sleeping in our canoes, we make a sign to be gone. The wildmen ask me to fire my gun, which makes a great noise, but no sooner do I let it off than we see seven canoes of Iroquois crossing toward land. We now see death before us. We are not strong enough to resist such a company, for they have 10 or 12 in every canoe. They see us and think we are more in number, so they hurry to make a fort. We persuade our wildmen to send seven canoes to an island near the fort. There they pass back and forth often to frighten our enemy by a show of force. Our wildmen have a mind to build a fort on that island, but we do not allow it. We prohibit them from cutting trees, so the enemy will not suspect our fear and our small number from the sound of our hatchets. We tell our people that to make a fort on land would only serve to put ourselves in prison. Thinking they are lost, our people obey us in everything. They say to us, "Be cheerful, and use us as you will, for we are dead men."

Meanwhile, the Iroquois enemies work lustily, thinking at every step that we will attack. They are far deceived, for if ever the blind wished for light, we wish for the obscurity of night.

No sooner does the night approach than we silently embark. It is strange that the enemy does not encounter us. We leave the Iroquois in their fort, and the fear in our breeches.

We paddle from Friday to Tuesday without stopping, with nothing to eat but a bit of salt meat. It is a pity to see our feet and legs bloodied from pulling our canoes up the swift rapids, over rocks with such sharp points. Nothing but the fear of death could make men do what we do.

We come to the Lake of the Beavers [Lake Nipissing of Ontario], and being in great hunger, we look for food. Some of us fish, some hunt. This done, we go down the River of the Sorcerers [French River of Ontario] which brings us to the first great lake [Lake Huron]. What joy we have to pass from that river, where we wrought 22 days without sleeping for a single hour on land.

Now being out of danger from our enemy, we must enter into another danger. We ready our equipage to wander upon that sweet sea, but most of the coast is void of wild beasts, so there is great

7

famine among us. Here I learn the kindness and charity of the wild-men, for when they find any fruit, they call my brother and me to eat and replenish our bellies. They show themselves far more grateful than many Christians.

I cannot forget here the finesse of one of these wildmen. He no sooner sees a beaver raise its head out of the water, than the wildman throws himself into the water and down to the bottom, without so much as giving notice. Before many of us know, he brings up the beaver in his arms like a child, without fearing to be bitten. By this we see that hunger can do much.

We now enter a strait 25 miles in length, full of islands, then proceed to a rapids [Sault Ste. Marie] separating the Upper Lake, which we call Superior. We make cottages and learn the truth of what the wildmen say—that once we arrive, we should make good cheer of a fish they call *assickmack*, or white fish.

The bear, the beaver and the elk appear often, and pay dearly for it. This is to us an earthly paradise. After fasting so long, after such great pains, we find ourselves able to choose our diet. Resting when we have a mind to rest, we taste pleasure for a sweet bit. (We do not ask for a good sauce; it is better to have it naturally. This is the way to distinguish the sweet from the bitter.)

But the season is far spent, and we leave that desired place in the hands of the cursed Iroquois. And yet if the Iroquois had the same liberty as in former days, we French could not have gone any further with our heads. We would not have known those great lakes so soon. Two men would not have learned so cheaply the truth of those seas. It is cheap when we need not put our hand to our purse. Yet we must pay out of civility. The wildmen pay: one giving thanks to the woods, another to the river, another to the earth, another to the rocks that stay the fishes.

The weather is agreeable as we begin to canoe on that great expanse of water . . . water so calm and air so clean. We go along the coast, most delightful and wonderful [the south coast of Lake Superior]. Nature has made it pleasant to the eye, the spirit and the belly. We see banks so high that when a wildman stands on one, he appears no more than a crow. It is a thing most incredible that the

8

waves of the lake should have such strength, to make the banks so high and the water so deep. There are very deep caves caused by their violence. This coast is most dangerous in a storm, there being no landing place. We must look to ourselves, and take time with our small canoes. When the lake is agitated, the waves go in the caves with such force that they make a horrible noise, like the shooting of great guns.

Some days later we come to the mouth of a small river [Portage River at Keweenaw Peninsula] where we kill some elk. We find meadows 25 miles square and smooth as a board. We go up the river 12 miles further and find ponds made by beavers. We must break the beaver dams to pass, and opening the sluice, it is wonderful to see the work of that animal which drowned more than 50 miles square and cut all the trees. Arriving at the river's source, we must drag our canoes over trembling ground for an hour. The ground trembles because the beavers have drowned great areas with dead water, whereon moss has grown two feet thick. Where I expect to go safe and dry, if I take not great care, I sink down to my head or the middle of my body. When I am out of one hole, I find myself in another. I am caught often. The wildmen warn me that when the moss breaks under, I should suddenly cast my whole body into the water, grab the moss and go like a frog, drawing my canoe after me. This saves me.

Having passed that place, we carry our canoes across the land for five miles. The way is well beaten by comers and goers, who, by making that portage, shorten their passage by eight days, crossing the point [Keweenaw Peninsula] that goes far into the lake. At the end of that point, I am told, there is an island of copper. This I have not seen.

We again embark on the lake and come to a river a quarter of a mile wide [Montreal River]. Many of our wildmen leave us to win the shortest way to their nation. Others join us in hopes of getting knives from us. They love knives better than we serve God, which should make us blush for shame.

We come to a bay 25 miles around [Chequamegon Bay]. In it there is a channel where we take a great store of fish: sturgeons of

9

vast bigness and pike seven feet long. At the end of this bay we land. The wildmen give thanks to that which they worship, we to the God of gods.

Here we must leave our navigation and forsake our canoes to a harder piece of work. The wildmen tell us we have five days journey to arrive where their wives are. We foresee the hard task of carrying our bundles upon our backs. They are used to it. It is everyone for himself, and God for all.

The wildmen fear that the Nadoneceronons [Sioux] have made war against their nation and have forced their wives from the appointed meeting place. My brother and I declare our will thus: "Brothers, we resolve to stay here, not being accustomed to make a carriage on our backs. You go and look for your wives. We will build a fort here. Seeing that you cannot carry all your merchandise at once, we will keep it for you, and will stay here 14 days. In that time you will send to us your wives, if they are alive. They will fetch what you leave and what we have. For their pains, we will give them gifts, and you will soon see us in your country. If your wives are dead, we will spend all to be revenged. We will gather up the whole country for the next spring, to destroy those who caused their death. You will see our strength and valor. Although there may be 7,000 fighting men in one village, you will see them flee. You will kill them to your best liking by the very noise of our weapons, and by our presence. We are the gods of the earth among those people."

They wonder very much at our resolution. The next day they go their way, while we set about to make a fort of stakes. We build a bastion in a triangle to defend us from an attack. The door is toward the water, the fire in the middle, and our covered bed on the right side. We lay boughs of trees one upon another around the fort, and we tie a long cord with small bells to act as our sentries. We finish the fort in two days.

As soon as we are lodged, I go to hunt while my brother keeps house. I am fittest to go, being youngest. I take my gun and go where I never was before. I go through a woods for some three or four miles, and I find a small brook, which brings me into meadows. There I find a pool with a good stock of wild geese. I begin to creep, thinking I am in Canada where the fowl are easily scared away; but these poor creatures, seeing me flat on the ground, think I am a beast like them. They come at me, whistling like goslings, trying to frighten me. The whistling that I make them hear is different music from theirs. I kill three and scare the rest, but they return to see what sudden sickness has befallen their comrades. I shoot again, and two pay for their curiosity.

We stay there 12 full days without any news, but we do have the company of wildmen from other nations, who come to us and admire our fort. We allow just one to come inside at a time, yet they often do not dare to come in—they fear our weapons so.

Our weapons are in good order, including five guns, two muskets, three fowling pieces, three pairs of great pistols, two pairs of pocket pistols, and each his sword and dagger. (We might say that a coward was not so well armed. Nevertheless, mistrust is the mother of safety, and the occasion makes the thief.)

During this time we have several alarms in the night. The squirrels, foxes and other small beasts come in and attack us. We imagine that some wildmen might surprise us, but I may say they are far more afraid then we.

I kill an elk, and I could kill more, but we like the waterfowl better. The wildmen bring us as much fish as we can eat, and more meat.

On the twelfth day we see far off some 50 young men coming toward us, some of them our former companions. We allow them to come into our fort, and they are astonished, calling us every foot devils to have built such a thing. They bring us food, thinking we are half starved, but they are mightily mistaken, for we have more than they are able to eat—60 geese and meat hanging from many sticks. We make good cheer. They stay three days, and during that time many of their wives arrive. We treat them well, for they seldom eat fowl, not knowing how to catch them except with arrows.

They offer to carry our baggage. We go away free of any burden, while those poor miserables are happy to carry our equipage, hoping that we will give them a brass ring, an awl or a needle.

We are Caesars, there being no one to contradict us.

11

Four hundred wildmen come to see us depart from that place. They admire our actions more than the fools of Paris admire the arrival of their king and his wife, the Infant of Spain. The fools of Paris cry out "God save the king and queen!" These wildmen make a horrid noise, and call to the gods and devils of heaven and earth.

FAMINE

Pierre Esprit Radisson   1658–59

*As winter set in, Radisson and Groseilliers lost all no-
tions of power or glory, and descended into a grim
struggle for survival.*

Snow begins to fall, warning us. Winter comes on.
We must retire from this place to seek our living
in the woods. Everyone gets his equipage ready.
So away we go, but not all to the same place. Two or three at
most go in any one direction. We do so because food is scant in
one place and cannot feed all.

But let us go where we will, we cannot escape the mighty hand
of God, who disposes as He pleases and who chastens us as a good,
a common, a loving father, not as our sins deserve.

Now we must live on what God sends, and war against the bears
in the meanwhile. (We want not bear's grease to anoint ourselves,
to run the better.) We beat down the woods daily to discover nov-
elties: elk, deer, buffalo, caribou and mountain cat—child of the devil.
We kill a few and live a good life.

But the snow increases daily. We make rackets [snowshoes], not
to play ball, but to exercise ourselves in a game harder and more
necessary. These are broad, so we may run over the snow and not
sink when we hunt the moose or other beast.

We come to a lake [Lac Court Oreilles in Sawyer County, Wis-
consin] where we find wildmen had arrived before us. We stay 14
days in this place, most miserable like a graveyard, for there falls so
much snow and frost with such a thick mist that all the snow sticks

13

Making snowshoes, by Frederic Remington

to the trees—pines, cedars and thorns. There is darkness upon the earth, as if the sun is eclipsed. The trees are so laden with snow that it falls as if sifted. On the ground the snow is not able to bear us, although we make snowshoes six feet long and a foot and a half wide. Often, trying to turn ourselves, we fall over and over again in the snow. If alone, we have trouble rising. By the noise we make, the beasts hear us from a great way off.

So famine is among many who did not provide for themselves beforehand, and who now must live on what they get each day. It grows worse and worse daily.

To increase our misery, we receive news that 150 Ottawas have had a quarrel with the Hurons. They come to make war against the

14

Hurons, hearing that the Hurons have knives and hatchets. We hope the Ottawas will bring us something for subsistence, but they are worse provided than we. They are reduced to famine.

Oh cursed covetousness! What will you do? Oh you poor people! You will have your booty, but you will pay dearly for it. You cry out for hunger. You women become barren and dry like wood. You men must eat the cord of the bow, because you have not strength to pull it. Children, you must die. Frenchmen, you who called yourselves gods of the earth to be feared, you too will taste this bitterness, and be too happy if you escape. Where are the times past? Where is the plenty that you had in all places and countries?

Daily there comes to us a new family of these poor people, half dead, having but skin and bones.

How can we have strength to make a hole in the snow for a bed, if we have not strength to haul our snowshoes after us, nor to cut a little wood for a fire to keep us from the rigor of the cold, which is extreme in this country?

Oh, if the music we hear could but give us pleasure, for we want not lamentable music nor grim spectacle. In the morning the husband looks upon his wife, the brother his sister, the cousin his cousin, the uncle his nephew, sometimes finding them dead. The living languish with cries and hideous noises that make the hair stand on our heads.

Good God, have mercy on so many poor, innocent people. Have mercy on us who acknowledge thee, who have offended thee and are punished. But we are not free of that cruel executioner.

Those who have any life search for roots. This is done with great difficulty, the earth being frozen two or three feet deep, with snow five or six feet above it. Our greatest subsistence is the rind tree [bittersweet] which grows like ivy about the trees. To swallow it, we cut sticks two feet long, tie them in a bundle and boil them. When they are boiled for one or two hours, the bark comes off easily. This we dry in the smoke, reduce into a powder between two stones, and put back in the kettle with the same water. This makes a kind of broth which nourishes us, but makes us thirstier and drier than the wood we eat.

15

In the first two weeks we eat our dogs. We go back over our steps to find bones and carcasses of beasts we have killed before. Happy is he who can find what another threw away, boiling it three or four times to get the substance out of it. We reduce to powder the bones—remains of crows and dogs. We put the powder half a foot in the ground and make a fire upon it. We cover it with earth, feeling the heat, then boil it again to give more froth than before. We take the animal skins from shoes, clothes and leggings, most of the skins from our lodges, even beaver skins where the children beshat more than a hundred times. We burn the hairs off the skins with coals. The rest goes down our throats. The wood is our food the rest of the time. We heartily eat these things most abhorred. We chew so eagerly that our gums bleed like fresh wounds.

Finally we become the very image of death. We often mistake ourselves, living for dead and dead for living. We lack strength to pull the dead out of lodges, and when we do, it is to put them four paces away in the snow. Here are more than 500 dead—men, women and children.

The wildmen, seeing my brother always in the same condition, say that some devil brings him food to eat. (The beard on his face hides his condition, but if they could see his body, they would know otherwise.) As for me with no beard, they say I love them because I live as poorly as they.

A great volume would not contain all the strange accidents that befall us. There come two men and a dog from a strange country. Our task is to catch the dog cunningly, for we know these people love their beasts. The dog is very lean and as hungry as we, but his masters do not suffer so much. These men are Nadoneseronons [Sioux]. They are so respected that nobody dares offend them, because we are upon their land. We offer them gifts, but they do not agree to trade. This makes me stubborn. In the night I go near their lodge. The dog comes out, for friendliness. I take him a little away and I stab him with my dagger. I bring him to our lodge, where he is broiled like a pig and cut in pieces, guts and all, so everyone in our family has his share. The snow where the dog is killed is not lost, because one of our family fetches it to season the kettle.

16

In the end, the wrath of God begins to appease itself. God pities His poor creatures. It is time to leave such miseries. Our bodies cannot hold out any more. Calm follows the storm, but calm kills us and storms favor us. Here come wind and rain, that put new life in us. This weather continues for three days. The forest clears. The snow hardens, and we no longer need snowshoes. Those with strings left in their bows take courage to use them. The small deer are caught in the crusted snow, as if by stakes. Now it is easy for us to take them and cut their throats with our knives.

We find ourselves a little nourished, yet we have not fully paid. Our guts, straightened by long fasting, cannot contain the food that we put in them.

We begin to look better daily. From the second day we begin to walk.

NATION
OF THE BUFFALO

Pierre Esprit Radisson   1659–60

*As Radisson and Groseilliers recovered from hunger,
they were visited by a delegation from the powerful
Sioux nation, whose homeland extended from the forests of northern Wisconsin far westward onto the Great
Plains. The Sioux had learned of the two Frenchmen
visiting their country—"strange men who speak with
thunder and make the earth quake."*

Here come eight ambassadors from the Nadoneseronons [Sioux], whom we call the Nation
of the Buffalo. Each man brings two wives
carrying wild rice, Indian corn and other grains for us. We receive
this as a great favor and token of friendship, but we would have
welcomed it a month or two earlier.

They make a great ceremony of greasing our feet and legs, and
we paint them with red. They strip us naked and put upon us robes
of buffalo and white beaver. They weep over our heads until we are
wet with tears. They make us smoke their pipes, not common pipes,
but pipes of peace and war. These they pull out but seldom, when
there is occasion for heaven and earth. To end the ceremony they
throw tobacco in the fire.

The next morning they are called by our interpreter. We understand not a word of their language. We sit on a higher place to

18

be at ease and to appear more in state. We borrow their pipe, made of red stone as big as a fist. The reed is five feet long and thick as a thumb. Tied to it is the tail of an eagle, spread like a fan and painted with colors. From the top of the reed hang feathers of ducks and other birds, all of fine colors. We remove the tail of the eagle, and in its place we hang 12 iron arrow tips, spread like feathers. We hang a knife from the reed, we plant a hatchet in the ground, and we surround their peace pipe with our weapons.

There is great silence. Everyone smokes his pipe.

We tell them, through our interpreter, "Brothers, we accept your gifts. You are summoned here to know our will and pleasure. First, we take you for our brothers by taking you into our protection. To show you this we replace the eagle's tail with our weapons, so that no enemy will approach this pipe of peace to break our bond." Then we lift up the 12 iron arrow tips, saying, "These points will pass over the whole world to destroy your enemies. Your enemies are our enemies." Then we pull the hatchet from the ground and turn about, saying, "We will kill those who war against you. We will make forts so you will come with more assurance to the Feast of the Dead."

We had prepared for this occasion some wet powder, the good powder being precious to us. We intended to make them believe this was our tobacco, to make smoke for them as they had made smoke for us. We throw the powder in the fire, but the powder has more strength than we think. Burning embers fly from one side of the lodge to the other. Hearing such a noise and seeing fire fly on every side, they run without looking for the door. They had never seen a sacrifice of tobacco so violent. We follow them to reassure them. We visit them in their lodges, where they receive us trembling with fear, believing that we are the devils of the earth.

There is nothing but feasting for eight days, and these men invite us to a greater feast—the Feast of the Dead.

When the time is near, we leave for the rendezvous between a small lake and a meadow [somewhere in eastern Minnesota]. When we arrive, most of our Ottawas have already arrived, and within three days several other nations arrive. When we number 500, we start

19

building a large fort. In two days the fort is finished, and can be seen from afar.

Soon 30 young men arrive—the scouts and foreguard of the Sioux nation. They carry nothing but bows and arrows, with arrow tips neatly made of pointed deer horns. They wear short garments, to be more nimble in chasing deer. They all are proper men, dressed with paint. They eat and rest for five hours without speaking. Then one of the Sioux warriors shoots an arrow, cries aloud and announces that the elders of their village will arrive the next day to renew old friendships, and to make new friendship with the French.

That night the Sioux are scattered in many lodges, expecting their comrades to come. Everything is made ready for them. A vast area is prepared some 100 paces from the fort for their tipis, which they carry upon their backs. Snow is moved aside, the ground is covered with pine boughs, and tent poles are planted.

The following day the Sioux arrive with incredible pomp. Their arrival reminds me of the entrance of the Poles into Paris, except that the wildmen have not so many jewels, but so many feathers.

First come the young men with bows and arrows. Small shields hang about their shoulders. The shields are covered with painted feathers representing all sorts of figures: the sun, the moon and beasts. The men's faces are dabbed all over with colors. Their hair is turned up like a crown and is cut even—or rather burned even, for fire is their scissors. They leave a tuft of hair on their crowns, tie it and bind it at the end with small pearls or turkey stones. They cover themselves with thick grease mingled with reddish earth, and with this stuff they make their hair stand up. They cover the crowns of their heads with swan's down or other white feathers. Their ears are pierced in five places with holes so big that a little finger can pass through. From their ears they hang ornaments of yellow copper in the shape of a star or a half moon. They are clothed lightly in elk or deer skins. Every one has a crow skin hanging from the girdle. They have pouches made of snake skins to which they tie bear paws or carvings from buffalo horn. Their leggings are embroidered with pearls and porcupine quills. They wear handsome shoes laced at the side of the heel with buffalo hair which trails for more than a half

20

a foot upon the snow. They carry swords and knives a foot and a half long, hatchets ingeniously made and wooden clubs like back-swords, some with round heads. About their arms they tie tufts of hair from enemies they have killed. Above all, they wear white robes of beaver skins.

Next come the elders, with great gravity and modesty, covered with buffalo robes that hang to the ground. Each carries in his hand a peace pipe set with jewels. Each has a sack on his shoulders that encloses all the world. Their faces are not painted, but their hair is dressed like the others.

Then come the women, loaded like so many mules. Their burdens make a greater show than they themselves, but I suppose the weight is less than the size. The women are conducted to the appointed place where they unfold their bundles and fling the skins that make their tipis. They build houses in less than a half hour.

The men rest, then come to the big meeting lodge. Fires are kindled. We arrive with great pomp, making four men carry our guns before us. We charge the guns with powder only; otherwise, with their lack of skill, they might kill their fathers. Each of us carries a pair of pistols, a sword and a dagger. We put rolls of porcupine-quill work around our heads, like crowns. They make a high place for us in the middle, knowing our custom. We have the men lay our weapons near us.

Four elders come with kindled peace pipe in hand. Four beautiful women bring bear skins to sit on. An old man throws the peace pipe at our feet. He thanks the sun for the day he saw the terrible men whose words make the earth quake. He sings awhile, then covers us with his robes. All naked except for his leggings, he tells us, "You are masters over us. Dead or alive, you have power over us and may dispose of us at your pleasure. You are masters of all things, of peace and of war."

They say they came to put themselves under our protection and to bring us back with them to their country. They present a gift of beaver skins, assuring us that the mountains in their country are leveled, the valleys raised, the ways smooth, the boughs of trees cut down, and bridges built over rivers so that we will not wet our feet.

21

Fur trader in the council tipi, by Frederic Remington

They say their villages and the lodges of their wives and daughters are open to us, because we keep them alive with our merchandise. A second gift they give to us is their promise of peace: to receive other tribes in their country, well pleased that they come to celebrate the Feast of the Dead. A third gift is their promise to open the gate of their fort, if necessary, to protect others from their enemy, the Christinos [Cree], who come to destroy them. They say they are men—the heavens made them so, obliging them to defend their country and their wives, the dearest things in the world. In all times their men have been strong and true soldiers, and they will show themselves so by meeting their enemy. They will not weaken, but will show by their actions that they are as valiant as their forefathers. A fourth gift is buffalo skins which they give to us, asking our help to defend their country. They know that the true means of victory is to have a thunder—they mean a gun, calling it a *miniskoick*.

So done, we rise, and one of us begins to sing. We tell them that we will save and keep their lives, taking them as brothers. As testimony we shoot all of our 12 gun, then draw our swords and long knives to our defense, putting the wildmen in such terror that they don't know whether to run or stay. We throw a handful of powder in the fire to make noise and smoke.

Our songs finished, we begin to work our teeth. We eat a kind of rice, much like oats. It grows wild in the water three or four feet deep. This is their food for most of the winter. For each man they put a handful in the pot, and it swells enough to suffice. By this bounty we see that there is a God that shows himself in every country, who is almighty, full of goodness, the preservation of those poor people who know him not.

This done, we go back to our fort as we came.

On the day following we ask the chiefs to come together, so we might answer their gifts. Our first gift is a kettle, to tell them that we have come from the other side of the great salted lake, not to kill them, but to make them live. The second gift is six hatchets, to tell them that we like men who generously defend themselves against their enemies. But we say that we, who are masters of peace and war, will dispose of affairs to see that the Sioux and the Cree join

23

together in peace. We say that the first nation to break this peace will be our enemy, and we will reduce them to powder with our heavenly fire. The third gift is two dozen knives, to lead them to a dance of union with the Cree. The fourth gift is six graters, two dozen awls, two dozen needles, six dozen looking glasses, a dozen little bells, six ivory combs and a little vermilion, to thank them for free passage through their country.

The Sioux shout a great "Ho! Ho! Ho!"—that is, thanks.

A company of about 50 Sioux are sent with me to visit the Cree. We arrive after three days [somewhere near the west end of Lake Superior]. All that day we feast, dance and sing. There are plays, mirths and battles for sport. In the public place the women dance as the elders beat drums and sing. The women hold flowers and dance modestly, not lifting their feet much from the ground, keeping their heads downward, making a sweet harmony. For a prize the young men try to climb a large post, 15 feet high, very smooth and oiled with bear and elk grease. They fight a mock battle, making war-like postures—discovering the enemy by signs, taking a prisoner or killing him and taking his head, pulling an arrow from the body, striking a shield with a club and knocking it to the ground. This is a furious thing, done without speaking, played to the beat of drums. These drums are earthen pots full of water, covered with deer skins.

We give them several gifts and we receive many, including 300 robes of beaver. Every one brings his most exquisite things to show what his country affords. They renew their alliances, make marriages, and honor the bones of their dead.

The Cree is a wandering nation with a vast country. In winter they live inland for hunting, in summer by the water for fishing. They clothe themselves with beaver skins in winter and with deer skins in summer. They are the best hunters in all America, scorning to catch the beaver in a trap. They do not kill young beavers, but leave them in the water, because they are sure they will catch them again. They do not burn their prisoners, but knock them in the head or slay them with arrows, saying it is not decent for men to be so cruel.

Spring approaches, which is the best time to kill the elk. A wild-man, my brother and I kill more than 600 elk and other beasts. We come to the lake side [Chequamegon Bay of Lake Superior] with great pains. We plan to wait for the ice to vanish, but we hear that the Ottawas have built a village on the point [Chequamegon Point] that forms the bay. We go toward it with all speed. We have a great store of booty which we do not trust to the wildmen, for the occasion makes the thief. We overload our sleds and pull them across the rotten ice. The farther we go, the stronger shines the sun. While still 12 miles from the point, we sink a half leg into the ice, yet we must advance, in spite of our chattering teeth. To leave our booty is to undo us. We strive so that I hurt myself and cannot stand or go farther. At this my brother leaves me with the two sleds to the keeping of God. I strip myself, cover myself with dry clothes and lie down on my sled. He hurries to the wildmen, where he learns the treachery of the Ottawas. Seeing us in extremes, they prescribe rules. He promises them what they ask, and they come to fetch me. For eight days I am so tormented that I think I will never recover. I rest neither day nor night. My brother rubs my legs with hot bear oil, keeping them well bound. After a while, I come to myself.

Now there comes a different company of wildmen, asking me to go with them. I prepare myself and go. We march for two days, but on the third day my sore breaks out again, and I can go no further. The wildmen leave me behind, although I have gone with them for their sake. I proceed forward the best I can, but I know not where, the sun being my only guide. I proceed for five days, sometimes finding old lodges where there is wood to make fires, and where I melt snow in my greasy cap. One night a fire breaks out in my lodge as I slumber, which awakens me in haste. Lame as I am, I must save my snow-shoes, shoes and leggings, which keep me alive. I fling them as far as I can in the snow. When the fire is out, I am forced to look for them in the dark, in the snow, all naked and very lame, almost starved from hunger and cold. But what is it that a man cannot do when he sees it concerns his life?

On the fifth day I hear a voice and I think it is a wolf. I stand still, until I see it is a man. (Many wildmen are up and down looking for me, fearing that the bears might devour me.) The wildman asks me if I am hungry. I say no, to show myself stout and resolute. He takes a pipe and 20 pounds of food out of his sack for me. We soon after find my brother with a band of Cree.

I cannot omit a strange encounter. A wildman comes to see us, and my brother shows him the image of Joseph, Holy Mary and the baby Jesus. Mary and Jesus are riding an ass, and Joseph is carrying a long cloak. My brother calls the animal a buffalo. The wildman is astonished. He weeps, pulls his hair, and tumbles about near the fire until he is in a sweat and wet with tears. At last coming to himself, he tells us we are devils who know all that is and ever was. He says he recognizes in the image his wife and child, who were taken by the Nation of the Buffalo four years ago. He takes the ass to be the Nation of the Buffalo, saying, "There I am with my long robe, seeking for my wife and child."

As we prepare to depart from the Upper Country, the Cree make gifts to us, asking that they come with us to Montreal. More than 400 Cree canoes bring us beaver pelts. Never before was seen such a company to go down to the French. It is a pleasure to see the embarking, for the young women go into the water stark naked, their hair hanging down. I think it is shameful, but they think it is an excellent and old custom. The women seek to animate the men to defend themselves valiantly, and so to return safely.

After two years of hardship in the wilderness, Radisson and Groseilliers returned to Quebec with a fortune in beaver pelts. There the French governor not only seized much of their new-found wealth, but also imprisoned Groseilliers, for embarking without the governor's permission. Radisson wrote, "The governor makes use of that excuse to do us wrong and to enrich himself with goods that we have paid for dearly, so he might better maintain his coach and horses in Paris."

Embittered by the French, Radisson and Groseilliers defected to the English, and helped them establish the Hudson's Bay Company. This enterprise competed against the French for the fur trade across much of Canada.

26

THIS ADORED STATION

Father Rene Menard   1660–61

*Certain Frenchmen soon entered the Upper Country
with motives other than wealth or power. They were
Catholic missionaries of the Jesuit Order, devoutly determined to convert the "pagan" Indians to Christianity. The first of the black-robed Jesuits to reach the
Upper Country was Father Rene Menard. In 1660 the
frail Menard, 56 years old, embarked from Quebec with
the spirit of a martyr, fully expecting to die. Upon his
departure, he wrote the following letter to his superior.*

In three or four months you may place me with the
memory of the dead, because of my age, my feeble
condition, and the rude life of those people. Yet I
feel such powerful instincts that, failing to take advantage of this
occasion, I would feel eternal remorse. I am overwhelmed with business. All that I can do is commend our journey to your prayers, and
embrace you with the same affection that I hope to greet you with
in eternity.

*The following account, written by Jean Làlemont, took
place at Keweenau Bay on the south coast of Lake
Superior.*

The poor father, eight Frenchmen, and their Ottawa guides started
in canoes from Trois Rivieres, Quebec, on August 28, 1660, and

arrived in the Ottawa country on October 15, after inconceivable labors, lack of food, and bad treatment from the Ottawas. The father, feeble and broken down with toil, could scarcely sustain himself. One Ottawa, a proud and vicious chief with four or five wives, treated the father very badly and ordered him out of his lodge, to build for himself a hut of pine boughs. Oh God! What a dwelling place in the rigors of winter.

Their food was scarcely better. Often it was a miserable boiled fish, to be divided among four or five, and this they owed to the charity that the savages bestowed upon one Frenchman, who waited on the shore for the return of the fishermen's canoes, like a poor beggar waiting for alms at the church door. Fish bones also served to amuse their appetites. There was nothing, not even pounded bones, that the poor, starving creatures could not use. A type of moss that grows on the rocks also served as food. They put it into boiling water, which formed a kind of foam or slime like that of snails. It served to nourish their imaginations rather than their bodies. The bark of oak, birch and basswood, well dried, pounded and mixed with fish oil, furnished them with excellent sauce. They ate acorns with greater pleasure than Europeans eat chestnuts. And yet there was never enough to satisfy their hunger.

Thus passed the first winter.

In spring and summer they fared better. They killed a few ducks, geese and doves, which provided excellent banquets. They picked raspberries and other small fruits.

As the second winter set in unexpectedly, the Frenchmen decided to fish like the savages, judging that hunger is more difficult than the risk of fishing. It was a pitiful sight to behold the poor Frenchmen in canoes, through rain and snow, tossed here and there by whirl-winds on this great lake, rolling like the sea. Often on returning they discovered that their hands and feet were frozen. Sometimes they were assailed by drifting snow, so the man steering could not see his companion in the bow of the canoe. Each time they landed safely, it seemed to be a miracle.

These poor Frenchmen, destitute of all that could refresh the body, were consoled by the grace of heaven. While the father was alive, they had holy mass every day, confessed themselves, and they received communion every eight days.

The father met with nothing but opposition to the faith from the savages, because of their brutality and polygamy. With little hope of converting these savages, he resolved to make a new journey of 250 miles, to instruct a band of poor Hurons, who had been chased by the Iroquois to the extremity of the world. The Frenchmen warned the father at once of the dangers to a poor old man—decrepit, weak and destitute of food—in making such a voyage. All this could not intimidate him. He had but one reply to his affectionate followers: "God calls me there. I must go, even though it costs me my life."

Father Menard wrote his last letter from Chequamegon Bay, just before he began his journey.

I would do myself great violence to descend from the cross that God has prepared me for in my old days, in this extremity of the world. There is not a single throb of my heart to revisit the settlement at Trois Rivieres. I do not know the nature of the rivets that hold me fast to this adored station, but the mere thought that some one may free me from it troubles me. I often awaken with a start, with the thought that there are no more Ottawas for me. I can say with truth that I feel more contentment here in a single day, in spite of cold, hunger and indescribable hardships, than I have ever experienced in any part of the world. The consolation that God has given me here has compelled me to acknowledge the prize of finding myself all alone among these barbarians, 1,300 miles from our French settlements.

Every day I hear of populous nations distant from here. I expect to die on my way to them, but I shall do all that is possible to reach them. I face three great obstacles: the route lies across swamps, through which you must feel your way and be in danger every moment of sinking too deep to free yourself; food can only be obtained by carrying it with you; and mosquitoes await in numbers that are frightful.

29

God will dispose of us according to his will, for life or for death. It will be a great blessing should our God call me to himself, from so good a station.

> *Shortly after writing this letter, Father Menard started his trek deeper into the wilderness. Somewhere on the headwaters of Wisconsin's Chippewa River, he was separated from his one French companion. Father Menard disappeared without a trace, in the depths of the north woods.*

SPIRITS

Father Claude Allouez   1666–67

In 1665 the mission that had claimed Father Menard's life was assigned to Father Claude Allouez. This Jesuit priest, young and resourceful, carried the Gospel to Chequamegon Bay on the south coast of Lake Superior. In his letters, Father Allouez described the religious beliefs of the natives. He reported that their world was alive with spirits, deities and demons.

There is a false and hateful religion, like the beliefs of some of the ancient pagans. The savages of these regions recognize no sovereign master of heaven and earth, but believe there are many spirits: some good, like the sun, moon, lake, river and woods; others evil, like the snake, dragon, cold and storms. Whatever seems helpful or hurtful, they call a *manitou*, and pay it the worship that we render only to the true God.

They appeal to these spirits whenever they go hunting, fishing, to war, or on a journey, by offering sacrifices to them. At the eat-all feast, which resembles a holocaust, a leading old man of the village acts as priest, haranguing the sun. In a loud voice he declares his thanks to the sun for lighting his way, to help him kill some animal. He exhorts the sun by this feast to continue its kind care of his family. During his plea, all guests eat to the last morsel. Then a man breaks a cake of tobacco and throws it into the fire. Everyone cries aloud as the tobacco burns and smoke rises aloft. With these cries the sacrifice ends.

31

I have seen an idol set up in the middle of a village. Among other gifts, the savages sacrificed ten dogs to it, so that this false god would send away a disease that was killing the people. Everyone went daily to make offerings to the idol. Besides public sacrifices, they have some that are private. Often in their lodges they throw tobacco into the fire, as an offering to their false gods.

During storms and tempests, they sacrifice a dog by throwing it into the lake. "This is to calm you," they say to the lake. "Keep quiet." At dangerous places in the rivers, they pacify the eddies and rapids by offering them gifts. They are convinced that they honor their false gods by this external worship, and those who are converted to Christianity observe these same rituals to the true God.

As these people are of gross nature, they recognize no purely spiritual god, believing that the sun is a man and the moon his wife; that snow and ice are a man who goes away in spring and comes back in winter; that the devil is in snakes, dragons and other monsters; that the crow, the kite and other birds are spirits that speak as we do; even that there are people among them who understand the language of birds, as some understand a little French. They believe the souls of the dead rule the fishes of the lake. From earliest times they have believed in the immortality and reincarnation of the souls of dead fishes. They never throw fish bones into the fire, for fear they might offend the souls, and the fish will no longer enter their nets. They hold in great awe a certain fabulous animal which they never see except in dreams, and which they call *Missibizi*. They recognize it as a great spirit, and offer it sacrifices to obtain good sturgeon fishing.

I must report here a strange event. After the death of a very old Potawatomi man, his relatives burned the body entirely to ashes, an act unlike the custom in that country. The reason was a legend. They believed that this old man's father was a hare, an animal that runs over the snow in winter; so the snow, the hare and the old man were relatives. The hare once told his wife that he disapproved of their children remaining in the depths of the earth, because they were relatives of the snow whose country is above, toward the sky. If ever they were put into the ground after their death, he would pray that

Medicine lodge, anonymous

the snow, his relative, would fall for so long and so deep that there would be no spring. Three years ago at the beginning of winter, the brother of this old man had died. After he was buried in the usual manner, snow fell so deep and winter lasted so long that people lost hope of seeing spring. All were dying of hunger, and no remedy could be found. The elders held many councils, but all in vain. The snow continued. Then one of them remembered the old threats of the hare. They dug up the dead man and burned his body. Immediately the snow stopped, and spring followed. Who would think that people could believe such absurd stories? Yet they regard them as true beyond dispute. They also say that little nuggets of copper they find at the bottom of the lake and in the rivers are the riches of gods who live in the depths of the earth.

The fountainhead of their religion is libertinism. Their sacrifices usually end in debauchery, indecent dances and shameful acts of concubinage.

They fast in honor of their ridiculous spirits, to learn some future outcome. I have seen men, planning for war or the hunt, pass a whole week eating nothing. They show such purpose that they will not stop their fast until they see in a dream that which they desire—perhaps a herd of moose or a band of Iroquois put to flight—not very difficult for an empty brain, exhausted from hunger and thinking all day of nothing else.

They believe that the most common cause of illness is failure to give a feast after success in fishing or hunting; that the sun, who takes pleasure in feasts, is angry with whoever fails in this duty, and so will make him ill. The most common remedy, and the most profitable for the sorcerer, is holding a feast to the sun, which takes pleasure in liberal actions.

They believe evil little spirits cause illness. These spirits are sent by an enemy, or they thrust themselves into the parts of the body most diseased. When someone has an aching head or arm or stomach, they say that a *manitou* has entered that part of the body and must be drawn or driven out. The most common remedy is to summon the sorcerer, who consults with the old men regarding the ailment. He then puts his mouth to the diseased part and, by sucking, pretends

34

to draw something from it. This may be a pebble, a bit of string, or something else which he has put into his mouth beforehand. He shows this object, saying, "There is the *manitou*. Now you are cured. It only remains to give a feast."

A young man was seized by a contagious disease, prevalent at the end of winter. He was an important man, so no kind of jugglery was spared for his cure. The sorcerer came to tell me that he had drawn from the sick man's body two dog's teeth. I told him, "That is not what causes his illness. Rather, it is the tainted blood in his body." I thought the man had pleurisy. The next day I baptized him in the name of St. Ignace, hoping that the great saint would confound the evil spirit and the sorcerer. Indeed, I bled him, and showing the blood to the sorcerer I said, "Here is what is killing this sick man. You should have drawn from him every drop of this corrupt blood, and not some alleged dog's teeth." But the sorcerer then made the sick man take a kind of medicine, which had an ill effect, and the patient laid as if dead for three hours. This result was proclaimed throughout the village, and the sorcerer, much surprised by the turn of events, confessed he had killed him and begged me not to forsake the poor man. The man was not forsaken by his patron, St. Ignace, who restored him to life and confounded the superstitions of those infidels.

35

I AM
THE DAWN

Bacqueville de la Potherie   1668–70

Among the few capable French agents who controlled vast areas of the Upper Country was Nicolas Perrot, whom the natives called Metamines *or "Little Corn." It was Perrot who made first contact with the Potawatomies, Mascoutens and Miamis. The narrative of those early encounters was written by Bacqueville de la Potherie, a friend of Perrot's.*

S ieur Perrot has rendered very important services to the colony. He has made known the glory of the king among the savages, and induced them to form alliances with us. On one occasion, among the Potawatomies, he was regarded as a god. He was curious to meet that nation, who dwelt at the foot of La Baye des Puants [Green Bay]. The French had been described to them as covered with hair, for the savages have no beards. The Potawatomies believed that the French were of a different species than other men. When they saw Perrot, they were astonished that he was made like themselves, and they regarded him as a celestial being—a gift from the sky and the spirits. The old men solemnly smoked a sacred pipe and came into his presence, offering the pipe to Perrot as homage. After he had smoked the pipe, it was presented to the tribesmen, who all blew tobacco smoke over him as if it were incense. They said to him, "You are one of the chief spirits because you use iron. It is for you to rule and protect all men. Praised be the sun, who has sent you to our country." They adored Perrot as a god. They took his knives and hatchets, and incensed them with the tobacco smoke from their mouths. They gave him so many kinds of food that he could not taste them all. "He is a spirit," they said. "This food that he has not tasted is not worthy of his lips." When he left the lodge, they insisted on carrying him upon their shoulders. They did not dare look in his face. The women and children watched him from a distance. The savage who had introduced him was treated as a captain.

Perrot was careful not to receive all these acts of adoration, although he did accept the honors so far as the interests of religion were not concerned. He told them he was not what they thought, but only a Frenchman. He said the real Spirit, who made all, has given to the French the knowledge of iron, and the ability to handle it. He said this Spirit wanted to show His pity for His creatures, and had permitted the French to settle in this country to remove the Potawatomies from the blindness in which they had dwelt. He said they had not known the true God, the author of nature, whom the French adore. Perrot said that once they established friendship with the French, the Potawatomies would receive all possible assistance. Perrot added that the fur of the beaver was valued by the French, and he wished to determine whether they could carry on trade.

The Potawatomies were so delighted with the new alliance that they sent messengers to inform the Illinois, Miamis, Outagamies [Fox Indians], Mascoutens and Kickapoos. The Potawatomies asked those tribes to visit and to bring beavers.

The Miamis, Mascoutens, Kickapoos, and 15 lodges of Illinois came toward Green Bay the following summer, and made their clearings 30 miles away, [near the site of Berlin, Wisconsin]. Those people had seen knives and hatchets, which induced them to associate with tribes who already had some union with the French. They sent envoys to ask the Potawatomies to visit them and to bring the Frenchmen. The Potawatomies were jealous when they saw that the French desired to go away with the envoys, so they told the French that those people had no beavers. Nevertheless, the French departed, and in five days they reached the vicinity of the village.

As the Frenchmen reached the bank of the river [Fox River], a dignified old man appeared with a woman, carrying a clay pot filled with cornmeal porridge. More than 200 strong, young men arrived, their hair adorned with headdresses, their bodies covered with black tattoos in many figures. They wore girdles and leggings of braided work. They carried arrows and war clubs.

The old man held a sacred pipe of red stone with a long stick, its whole length decorated with flame-colored heads of birds, and in the middle, a bunch of bright red feathers like a great fan. When he saw Perrot, he gave him the pipe, from the direction of the sun. He uttered words to all the spirits whom those people adore. He held the pipe toward the east, toward the west, then toward the sun. He stuck the end in the ground, then turned the pipe around him as if pointing out the whole earth, making Perrot understand that he had compassion toward all men. Then he rubbed Perrot's head, back, legs and feet, and sometimes his own body. This welcome lasted a long time, while the old man made a harangue, like a prayer, to assure Perrot of their joy at his arrival.

One of the men then spread on the grass a large, painted buffalo hide, with hair as soft as silk, on which Perrot sat. The old man rubbed two pieces of wood together to make fire, but because the wood was wet, he could not light it. Perrot then drew forth his fire-steel and immediately made fire with tinder. The old man uttered loud cries about the iron, which seemed to him a spirit. The pipe was lit, and each man smoked. Then they ate porridge and dried meat, and they sucked the juice of green corn. Again the pipe was filled, and they blew tobacco smoke into Perrot's face, as the greatest honor they could render him. Perrot was smoked like meat, but said not a word.

The next day Perrot gave them gifts and made the following speech, suited to their character: "I admire your young men. Although, since their births, they have seen only shadows, they seem as fine-looking as those born in countries where the sun always shines. I would not have believed that the earth, mother of all men, could have provided you the means of survival when you did not have the light of the French. You will become another nation when you know us. I am the dawn of that light, which is beginning to appear in your lands; which precedes the sun; which will shine brightly and will cause you to be born again, in another land, where you will more easily find all necessities in greater abundance."

"I see this fine village, filled with young men as courageous as they are well built. They will not fear their enemies if they carry French weapons. I leave my gun for these young men. They must regard it as the pledge of my esteem for their valor. They must use it if attacked. It will serve them better in hunting buffalo and other beasts than all their arrows. I leave my kettle to you, old men. You will carry it everywhere without fear of breaking it. You will cook in it the meat that your young men bring from the hunt, as well as the food you will offer to Frenchmen who come to visit." Perrot tossed a dozen awls and knives to the women and said to them, "Throw away your bone awls. These French awls will be much easier to use. These knives will be more useful in killing the beaver and cutting meat than the pieces of stone you now use." He threw to them some beads and said, "See. These will better adorn your children and girls."

The Miamis excused themselves for not having beaver skins to give to Perrot in return. Until that time they had roasted those animals.

So this alliance began, through the agency of Sieur Perrot. A week later the savages gave a solemn feast, to thank the sun for having led Perrot to their village. In the lodge of the great chief of the Miamis an altar was erected, on which they placed a *pindiikosan*. This is a warrior's pouch, filled with medicinal herbs wrapped in the skins of animals, the rarest that they can find. It contains all that inspires their dreams. Perrot, who did not approve of this altar, said that he adored a God who forbade him to eat things sacrificed to evil spirits, or to the skins of animals. They were greatly surprised at this, and asked if Perrot would eat if they shut up their spirits. This he agreed to do. The chief begged Perrot to consecrate him to Perrot's God. The chief said that he would prefer Perrot's spirit,

Talon at the Pageant of the Sault, by Robert Thom

because his own spirit had not taught them how to make hatchets, kettles, and all else that men need.

> *The next year Perrot returned to Green Bay, to convince the natives to send envoys to Sault Ste. Marie. There the French planned to stage a pageant, at which they would take possession of the Upper Country for the King of France.*

It was in the interest of the colony to make known the glory of the king among all the peoples of the north, the west, and the south. In 1670 Monsieur Talon, intendant of Canada, set out with Sieur Perrot, who was considered the most able man to conduct this business. They had orders to take possession of all the country of the Outaouaks [Ottawas]. The Sault Ste. Marie was the place where councils of all the tribes were held, so this was the place where the matter could be transacted with the most pomp.

Perrot arrived at Green Bay in May. It was necessary to interest the Foxes, Miamis, Mascoutens, Kickapoos and Illinois in the plan. The Potawatomies escorted him to their village. When Perrot was ten miles distant from the village, he sent word of his arrival. The chief of the Miamis immediately gave orders to go in war-like array to receive Perrot. At once they marched, in battle order, decked with handsome feathers, and armed with quivers, bows, arrows and clubs. They marched in single file, their clubs uplifted, uttering yells. The Potawatomies, seeing their advance, told Perrot that the Miamis were receiving him in martial fashion, and that he must imitate them. Immediately Perrot placed himself at the head of the Potawatomies, and they rushed upon the Miamis, with their guns loaded with powder. The file of the Miamis passed to the left and made a circuit of 500 paces, in order to surround them. The head of the file joined the rear, and the Potawatomies found themselves hemmed in. The Miamis, uttering a terrible yell, suddenly came pouring upon them, firing arrows above their heads. When they were almost near enough to deal each other blows, the Miamis came on as if to attack them with their clubs. The Potawatomies made frightful cries and fired a volley from their muskets. Then all mingled together. Such was the reception by those people, who with peace pipes in hand, then escorted their guests to their village.

Several days later, the chief of the Miamis commanded his people to entertain Perrot with a game of la crosse. More than 2,000 savages assembled on a great plain, each with his racket. A wooden ball was thrown into the air, and all that could be seen was flourishes of all the rackets. They made a noise like that of weapons in battle. Half of the savages tried to send the ball toward the northwest the length of the plain; the others tried to send it to the southeast. The result of the strife, which lasted half an hour, was doubtful. Games of this sort often result in broken heads, arms and legs.

At the end of May, the chiefs of Green Bay, those of Lake Huron and Lake Superior, as well as the people of the north and several other tribes all came to the Sault. A stake was planted, and gifts were made to them on behalf of His Majesty, the king. They were asked to acknowledge our king, who offered them his protection. All the chiefs replied that they held nothing dearer than the alliance with the French and their special regard for the great chief who lived beyond the great lake. Sieur Perrot then announced to them, "I take possession of this country in the name of him whom we call our king. This land is his. All these people who hear me are his subjects, whom he will protect as his own children. He desires that they live in peace. He will take in hand their affairs. He will destroy any enemies who rise up against them. If his children have any disputes among themselves, he desires to be the judge."

Talon then attached to the stake an iron plate on which the coat of arms of the king were painted. He drew up an official report, and he made all the peoples sign it. The chiefs, for their signatures, drew the insignia of their families. Some drew a beaver, others an otter, a sturgeon, a deer or an elk. Other reports were drawn up, and one was slipped under the iron plate. It remained there only a short time, for hardly had the crowd separated when the savages drew the nails out of the plate, threw the document into a fire, and again fastened up the coat of arms of the king. They feared that the written paper was a spell, which would cause the deaths of all people who lived in that country.

PARADISE

Father Claude Dablon 1670–71

In September of 1670, Father Claude Dablon, a Jesuit priest, entered "paradise" on what is now the Upper Fox River of east-central Wisconsin. The Upper Fox flowed gently through beds of wild rice, past beautiful prairies spotted with lovely groves of wide-crowned oaks, and teeming with game. But before Father Dablon arrived at this paradise, he had to ascend the treacherous Lower Fox.

This country has the beauty of an earthly paradise, but we may say that the route to this paradise is as trying as the way to heaven provided by our Lord. We advance scarcely one day's journey on the river [Fox River] at the end of La Baye des Puants [Green Bay], when we find eight or ten miles of rapids, more difficult than the rapids in other rivers. To drag our canoes, we must walk over flints so sharp and cutting that we have all the trouble in the world to steady ourselves against the great rushing of the water.

At a fall of these rapids we find an idol honored by the savages. It is a rock formed naturally in the shape of a man: the head, shoulders and breast, but much more the face, which the savages paint with their most handsome colors. In ascending, the savages never fail to make some sacrifice of tobacco, arrows, paintings, or other things, to thank the idol for his help. If they must descend, they pray to him to help with their perilous navigation. We remove this cause

43

of idolatry, lifting the idol by the strength of our arms and throwing him into the depths of the river, to appear no more.

As a reward for passing this way, rough and dangerous, we enter into the most beautiful country ever seen—prairies on all sides, as far as the eye can reach, separated by this river flowing gently through them. We see small hills with groves of trees here and there, as if planted to shade the traveler from the ardent heat of the sun. To paddle on this river is to repose oneself.

Here are elms, oaks and similar trees, but none with bark suited to cover cabins or make canoes. For this reason, these savages do not go on the water, and they have houses made of rushes bound together in mats. Grape vines, plum trees and apple trees are seen in passing, and invite the traveler to stop and taste their fruits, which are very sweet and abundant. All the borders of this river, flowing tranquilly through the prairies, are thick with wild rice, of which the birds are wonderfully fond. Game is so abundant that we kill it without stopping. With such diversions, one does not tire of floating on these lakes and rivers.

This country is all prairie for many leagues around. Among these rich pastures are found buffalo, which the savages call *pisikiou*. The savages use buffalo hides as robes and fur linings to protect themselves against the cold. The buffalo's flesh is delicious. Its fat mixed with wild rice makes the most delicate dish in this country.

This same river is interrupted by many little lakes, in which are seen certain peculiar, rare birds, which the savages call "chete" [white pelicans]. One would think, from a distance, that they are wild swans with their white plumage, their long necks and feet, and their large bodies. The difference and the rarity is the bill, more than a foot in length and thick as an arm. Each bird rests its bill on its neck, to relieve itself of the weight. Under this bill is a sack of delicate and pliable skin, which when closed is gathered up so neatly that nothing appears. But when the time comes, the bill can be opened so wide that a man's head could fit into it easily. Swimming against the fish and spreading this sack, the bird causes the fish to go into it like a net. God has taught men to fish by the lesson of these natural fishers.

On this river, the savages take game and fish together. Seeing that ducks, teal and other birds search the water in autumn for grains of wild rice, they spread their nets so skillfully that in one night they sometimes take as many as 100 pieces of game, not counting the fish. It is a pleasure to see a duck taken close to a pike, and carp entangled in the same threads with teal. The savages nourish themselves with this manna for about three months.

Nature and necessity have given them another invention in the same river, five miles from its mouth. It is made so that a child may be an excellent fisher. They bar the river from one side to the other with a palisade of stakes planted in the water. The hurdles allow water to flow through, but stop the large fish. Along this barrier they build scaffolds on which they wait in ambush. When fish follow the current and arrive at this barrier, the fisherman casts a pocket-shaped net and he easily catches fish. These two kinds of fishing draw savages from all parts to this place.

The bear and the racoon fill the country. These animals and the deer are easily hunted in the woods, which are very clear and contain large prairies. An animal often throws itself into the river, where one may take it without trouble.

Green Bay is the great passage of all the neighboring Indian nations, who have continual trade among themselves. We have decided to build our chapel here, in the center of more than ten different nations who can provide more than 15,000 souls to be instructed in the truths of Christianity. Here Father Claude Allouez and Father Louis Andre worked for the salvation of the people. The fathers have separated themselves, one appealing to the nations removed in the woods, the other to the nations near the Lake of the Puants [Lake Winnebago].

The natives here recognize diverse divinities to whom they make sacrifices. They have gods as the pagans had, in the heavens, in the air, on earth, in the woods, in the waters, and even in hell. The sun and the thunder they recognize as gods of heaven and air. Each beast, fish and bird has a particular spirit who cares for it, who preserves it and defends it from the evil which anyone would do to it.

These people have a peculiar consideration for animals, as for a mouse we had thrown out of doors. A girl seized it and wanted to eat it, but her father first took the mouse and gave it a thousand caresses. We asked him why. He said, "It is to appease the spirit who cares for the mice, so he will not distress my daughter."

To certain spirits they render far more respect than others, because the animals are more useful. One cannot believe the veneration they have for the bear, for when they have killed one, they make a solemn feast with very particular ceremonies. They carefully preserve the head of the bear. They paint it with the most handsome colors they can find. During the feast they put it in a place of honor, there to receive the adoration and praise of all guests, in their finest songs, one after another.

These savages go four and five days without eating so that, having weakened the mind, they may see in a dream one of these spirits. They believe they cannot succeed in hunting the deer or bear unless they have seen them in dreams, so all their care before the hunt is to see the beast they desire. They prepare themselves by the greatest fasts, which they sometimes prolong as long as ten days. This is done more often by the Renards [Fox Indians]. They do far more, for when the men are at the hunt, they compel the little children to fast, in order to dream of the bear that their parents seek. They believe the beast will be taken if it is once seen in a dream, even by the children. They have many other superstitions which challenge a missionary, who has all these monsters to combat at once.

Father Andre had already attacked them on their lives and superstitions during the several months he passed with them last summer. Willing to occupy the winter there, he set off on December 15th to go there by rough and dangerous routes. Locked in by ice on the bay and wanting to shorten the distance, he made his way from point to point. Toward evening when he wished to reach land he found that the passage was closed by mountains of ice, piled one on another, forming a rampart impossible to pass through. The sun set before he could find an escape. The father cast his eyes on some piles of ice blocks, in the midst of which he planned to pass the night, but happily he was inspired not to rest there, for these mountains of ice were carried off by the wind as night came on. He found a safer retreat on a point of land extending into the lake, and he stayed there, without danger of perishing, but suffering extreme cold. He had to keep this post for three days. Then, with a north wind following a rain, the lake became a complete sheet of ice, so smooth it was difficult to walk without falling at every step. He even found himself in the midst of a number of holes in the ice. He escaped, nevertheless, dragging himself among these precipices, until he reached the savages. One of the chiefs, to regale him after so much toil, offered him a sack full of acorns. This was not to be refused, for it was no small present among those people, who have no food more delicious during the winter, when hunting and fishing do not succeed.

The first concern of the father was to visit all the lodges to teach the children, and to apply the mysteries of our religion. The days were too short to satisfy the holy curiosity of those people. They did not allow him time to take his meals until very late, nor to perform his devotions, except in some retired place where they continued to seek him. They eagerly sought to hear the spiritual songs with French airs that he sang to the children. On the pathways and in the lodges, our mysteries were made public, were received with cheers, and were stamped on their minds by means of these canticles. This success gave courage to the father, and he resolved to attack the men through the children, to combat their idolatry with these innocent souls. He composed canticles against the superstitions and vices most opposed to Christianity. He taught these canticles to the children by the sound of a soft flute. He then went everywhere with his little savage musicians, declaring war against the sorcerers, the dreamers and those with many wives. And because the savages passionately love their children and suffer everything from them, they allowed the biting reproaches made through songs from the mouths of their children.

This gave the father much joy. He saw that God made use of these innocent mouths to confound the impiety of their own parents.

GREAT
RIVER

Father Jacques Marquette   1673

Indians who visited Chequamegon Bay on Lake Su-
perior in 1670 told the Jesuit Father Jacques Marquette
about a mighty river flowing south through the wil-
derness. Marquette wrote, "When the Illinois come to
Chequamegon, they pass a great river that is two miles
wide. It runs so far to the south that the Illinois have
not heard of its mouth. It is hardly credible that this
large river empties at Virginia, and we rather believe
that it has its mouth in California. If the savages make
me a canoe, we shall travel on this river as far as
possible." In 1673 Father Marquette joined the expe-
dition of explorer Louis Jolliet, to discover the river the
Indians called "Mississippi," or Great River. They em-
barked from Mackinac in two canoes, and followed
the west coast of Lake Michigan southward toward
Green Bay.

I put our voyage under the protection of the Blessed
Virgin Immaculate, promising her that if she did us
the grace to discover the great river, I would give it
the name "Conception." With these precautions, we made our paddles play merrily over the Lake of the Illinois [Lake Michigan].

The first nation we met was the Folles Avoine [Menominee], and
I entered their river [Menominee River]. The wild rice, from which

48

they take their name, is a kind of grass which grows spontaneously in little rivers with muddy bottoms, and in marshy places. It rises above the water in June, and keeps rising until September. Savages then go in canoes across the fields of wild rice, and shake the ears on their right and left into the canoe as they advance.

I told the Menominees of my plan to discover distant nations, to instruct them in the mysteries of our holy religion. The Menominees were very much surprised and did their best to discourage me. They said I would meet nations that never spare strangers, but tomahawk them without reason; that I might be killed by war parties that are constantly in the field; that the Great River is very dangerous, full of frightful monsters who swallow up men and canoes together; that there is even a demon there who can be heard from afar, who engulfs all who dare approach; and that the heat is so great in those countries that it would cause our death.

I thanked them for their kind advice, but assured them I could not follow it, because the salvation of souls was at stake. I said that for those souls, I should be too happy to lay down my life. I added that we would defend ourselves well enough against the river monsters.

We soon after reached the extremity of the La Baye des Puants [Green Bay] where our fathers labor in the conversion of those tribes. We left Green Bay to enter a river [Fox River]. This river is very beautiful at its mouth—full of geese, ducks, teal and other birds attracted there by the wild rice. But when you advance a little up this river, it becomes very difficult—full of strong currents and sharp rocks.

We arrived at a village of Mascoutens, Miamis and Kickapoos [near the site of Berlin, Wisconsin]. This was the limit of the discoveries made by the French, for they had not yet passed beyond it. When I visited those tribes I was most comforted to see a beautiful cross planted in the middle of their village, adorned with white skins, red belts and bows and arrows, which these people had offered to the Great Manitou (such is the name they give to God) to thank him for having had pity on them during the winter, sending them plenty of game when they were in greatest fear of famine.

49

Birch bark for lodges is rare in this country, so these people use mats of rushes which serve them for walls and roof, but are no great shelter against the wind, and still less against the rain when it falls in torrents. The advantage of this kind of lodge is that they can roll up the mats and carry them in hunting season.

The next day, the 10th of June, two Miami guides embarked with us in sight of a great crowd, who wondered to see just seven Frenchmen in two canoes dare to undertake so strange and hazardous a voyage. We knew that just 70 miles from the Mascoutens there was a river called Meskousing [Wisconsin River] that empties into the Mississippi. We knew that we must hold to the west-southwest point of the compass to reach it, but the way [on Fox River] was so cut up by marshes and little lakes that it would be easy to go astray, especially when the river was so covered with wild rice that you could hardly discover the channel. So we had a good need of our two savage guides, who led us safely to a portage [now the site of Portage, Wisconsin]. They helped us carry our canoes to Wisconsin River, after which they left us alone, in an unknown country, in the hands of Providence.

Here we leave the waters which flow toward Quebec, to follow those which will lead us into strange lands.

Wisconsin River is very broad, with a sandy bottom forming many shallows which render navigation difficult. It is full of vine-clad islands. On the banks appear fertile lands varied by woods, prairies and hills. We saw oak, walnut, basswood and another kind of tree armed with long thorns. We saw no small game or fish, but we did see deer and elk in considerable numbers.

After 100 miles on this river, we reached the mouth of the Great River. We safely entered the Mississippi on the 17th of June, with a joy I cannot express.

We gently followed the Mississippi southward, seeing deer and buffalo, geese and swans. From time to time we came upon monstrous fish, one of which struck our canoe with such violence that I thought it was a great tree about to break our canoe to pieces. We also saw in the water a monster with the head of a tiger and the sharp nose of a racoon, with whiskers and straight, erect ears. When

Bluffs on the Upper Mississippi, by George Catlin

we reached the latitude of 41 degrees 28 minutes, we found that turkeys took the place of other game, and buffalo took the place of other animals.

The buffalo are very fierce. Not a year passes without them killing savages. When attacked, they catch a man on their horns if they can, throw him into the air, throw him to the ground, trample him under foot, and kill him. If a hunter shoots at them with bow or with gun, he must immediately throw himself down and hide in the grass, for if they see him, they will attack.

We continued to descend the Great River, not knowing where we were going. We kept on our guard, making only a small fire toward evening to cook our meals, and spending the night in our canoes, anchored on the river.

Finally, on June 25th, we saw at the water's edge the tracks of men and a narrow path leading to a fine prairie. Monsieur Jolliet

51

and I silently followed this path for five miles and came to three villages near the bank of a river [Iowa River or Des Moines River]. We heartily commended ourselves to God, imploring his aid, and we approached so near we could hear the savages talking. We then decided it was time to reveal ourselves, and we did so by shouting with all our energy. The savages [Illinois Indians] quickly issued from their lodges and probably recognized us as Frenchmen, especially when they saw a "black gown" [Jesuit priest].

Four old men approached us, two of them bearing peace pipes. As they walked, they slowly raised their pipes to the sun. They then led us toward the door of a lodge where an old man awaited us in a surprising attitude. He stood erect and stark naked, with his hands extended and lifted toward the sun, as if to protect himself from its rays, which nevertheless shone upon his face through his fingers. He said to us, "How beautiful the sun is, oh Frenchmen, when you come to visit us. All our village awaits you, and you shall enter all our lodges in peace." A crowd of people devoured us with their eyes, but observed profound silence.

We then went to the village of the great chief, whom we saw at the door of his lodge, between two old men, all three erect and naked, and holding their pipes turned toward the sun. The chief said, "I thank you, black gown, and you, oh Frenchman, for taking so much trouble to come visit us. Never has the earth been so beautiful or the sun so bright as today. Never has our river been so calm or so clear of rocks, which your canoes have cleared away in passing. Never has our tobacco tasted so good. Never has our corn appeared so fine. Here is my son, whom I give to you to show you my heart." Having said this, he placed a little slave near us and gave us an altogether mysterious pipe. He then begged us to go no further on the Mississippi because of great dangers. I replied that I did not fear death, and that I regarded no happiness greater than that of losing my life for the glory of God. This they could not understand.

The following day we left, promising to pass that village again within four moons. Before quitting the Illinois country, I should relate their customs, which I observed.

52

When they say "Illinois," it means "the men," as if other savages
are merely animals. They are active and very skillful with bows and
arrows. They also use guns, which they buy from savages who trade
with the French, to terrorize their enemies with noise and smoke.
Their enemies, who live toward the west, have never seen guns. The
Illinois are warlike and are dreaded by distant tribes to the south
and west, where they go to capture slaves. They sell these slaves to
other nations at a high price in exchange for wares. The Illinois paint
their faces with red ochre. They live by hunting game, plentiful in
that country, and by growing Indian corn, of which they always have
a good crop. They also grow beans, melons and squash. Their lodges
are very large, roofed and floored with mats made of rushes. They
make utensils out of wood and ladles out of buffalo skulls.

Nothing among the Illinois is more mysterious or more esteemed
than the sacred pipe. They honor it more than Europeans honor the
crowns and sceptres of kings. The pipe seems to be their god of
peace and war, their arbiter of life and death. If you carry it about
and show it, you can march fearlessly amid enemies who will lay
down their arms when it is shown, even in the heat of battle. The
Illinois gave me a pipe to serve as my safeguard among the nations
I had to pass on my voyage.

There is a pipe for peace and a pipe for war, distinguished only
by the colors of the feathers which adorn them. Red is the sign of
war. The pipe is made of a polished red stone, like marble, fastened
to a stem which is two feet long and thick as a cane. It is decorated
with the heads and necks of different birds with beautiful plumage,
as well as large feathers of red, green and other colors. They esteem
the pipe especially, because they regard it as the pipe of the sun. In
fact, they present the pipe to the sun when they wish to obtain calm,
or rain, or fair weather. They will not bathe at the beginning of
summer, nor will they eat new fruit, until they have danced the pipe.

The pipe dance is famous among these people. A place of honor
is made for the god of the person who gives the dance, which they
call a *manitou*. This is a snake, a bird, or something else which they
have seen in a dream. All come to sit in a circle under the trees, but
each on arriving must salute the *manitou* by blowing smoke on it.

53

He who begins the dance offers the pipe to the sun: he tips it toward the earth, spreads its wings as if to fly, and puts it near the mouth of those present. He then makes a sign to another warrior to take arms, and invites him to fight to the sound of drums. The warrior takes up bow and arrows and the war hatchet, and begins a duel with the other, whose sole defense is the pipe. One attacks, the other defends; one strikes blows, the other parries; one takes flight, the other pursues; then he who was fleeing faces about and makes his opponent flee. This spectacle is done so well, with slow and measured steps to the cadence of voices and drums, that it might pass for the opening of a very fine ballet in France.

We took leave of the Illinois in late June, and continued to descend the Mississippi. Some days later, while skirting some high rocks, we saw two painted monsters which frightened us at first [at the site of Alton, Illinois]. Each was large as a calf, with horns like a deer, a horrible look, red eyes, a beard like a tiger's, a face like a man's, a body covered with scales, and a long tail that passes above the head and goes back between the legs, ending in a fish tail. These two monsters are painted so well, in red, green and black, that we could not believe a savage was the artist. As we talked about these monsters and paddled quietly in clear and calm water, we heard the noise of rapids ahead. I have seen nothing more dreadful. A tangle of large trees, branches and floating islands was issuing from the mouth of a river called Pekistanouis [Missouri River] with such force that we passed it with great danger. So great was the agitation, that the water became very muddy and did not become clear again.

After making about 50 miles due south, and a little less to the southeast, we came to a river called Ouaboukigou [Ohio River]. This river comes from the country to the east, inhabited by people called Chaouanons [Shawnee] who have as many as 38 villages. They are by no means warlike.

Here we began to see canes growing on the banks of the river. They are a beautiful green, with narrow, pointed leaves. They grow very tall, and so thick that the buffalo have trouble passing through them.

54

We soon entered mosquito country. To shelter ourselves from the mosquitoes and from the sun, we used our sails to make a sort of cabin on the water. Thus we were borne along at the will of the current.

We began to see less prairie land, because both banks of the river were lined with lofty trees. The cottonwood, elm and basswood were admirably tall. Yet we still heard buffalo bellowing, which made us think the prairies were near. We saw quails at the water's edge, and we killed a little parrot with a red head, a yellow neck and a green body.

We descended to near 33° latitude where we saw a village of savages called Mitchigameas. Here we prayed to our patroness and guide, the Blessed Virgin Immaculate. We needed her aid, for soon we heard yells from afar as the savages were exciting one another to combat. They were armed with bows, arrows, axes, war clubs and shields. They prepared to attack us by land and by water. Some embarked in large wooden canoes to cut off our way, and to surround us. Those on shore kept going and coming, as if to attack. Some of the young men jumped into the water to seize my canoe, but the current forced them to return to shore. One of them threw his war club at us, and it passed over our heads. I showed the peace pipe and made gestures of peace, but their alarm continued. They were about to pierce us with arrows from all sides when God suddenly touched the hearts of the old men on the waterside. Doubtless they had not seen our peace pipe from a distance; but when they recognized it they were touched, and they restrained their young men. Two of the chiefs threw their bows and quivers into our canoes. They then took us to shore where we disembarked, but not without fear.

At first we had to speak by signs, for they did not understand any of the six languages I knew. At last an old man was found who spoke a little Illinois. We showed them that we were going to the sea. They understood perfectly; but I knew not whether they understood what I told them of God and of the things which concerned their salvation. My words were a seed cast in the earth, which will bear its fruit in season.

55

Jolliet and Marquette at the great village of the Illinois, by Robert Thom

They told us we would learn all we desired at another great village of people called Akamsea [Arkansas], only 25 miles farther down the river.

The next morning we embarked. About a mile from the Arkansas village we saw two canoes coming toward us. The chief was standing up, holding a peace pipe with which he made signs to us. As he approached us, he was singing quite agreeably. He invited us to smoke, after which he gave us some bread made of Indian corn.

We then asked the Arkansas what they knew of the sea. They said we were but ten days' journey from the sea. They did not know what nation of Europeans lived there, because their enemies—savages who used fire-arms—had cut off their passage, and had kept them from trading with the Europeans. They warned us that if we went any further, we would expose ourselves to war parties which their enemies continually sent out on the river.

Monsieur Jolliet and I held council to decide what we should do—whether we should push on or rest satisfied with the discovery we had made. We believed that we were not far from the Gulf of Mexico, in which the Mississippi undoubtedly has its mouth. (We realized the Mississippi could not have its mouth to the east, in Virginia, because we had already passed south of the latitude of the Virginia seacoast without having reached the sea. Nor could the Mississippi have its mouth to the west, in California, because we had been traveling only southward). We knew, moreover, that we would lose the fruit of our voyage if we threw ourselves into the hands of the Spaniards at the Gulf of Mexico. They would hold us as prisoners, and we would not be able to return with our information. Besides, it was clear that we could not resist savages who were expert in the use of fire-arms, and who infested the lower part of the river. We had gathered all the information that could be desired, so we resolved to return. After a day's rest, we prepared for the return trip.

After announcing the Gospel as well as I could to the Arkansas, we left their village on the 17th of July to retrace our route. We ascended the Mississippi, which gave us great trouble in stemming its currents.

57

At the 38th parallel we entered another river [Illinois River] which greatly shortened our route, and took us with little effort to Lake Michigan. We have seen nothing like this river for its fertile soil, its prairies and woods, its buffalo, elk, racoons, geese, swans, ducks, parakeets and even beaver.On this river we found a village of Illinois called Kaskaskia, consisting of 74 lodges [near the site of Utica, Illinois]. One of the chiefs with his young men escorted us to Lake Michigan [via the portage at Chicago]. At the end of September we reached Green Bay.

If my perilous journey has been attended with no other advantage than the salvation of one soul, I would think my perils sufficiently rewarded.

FATAL
WINTER

Father Jacques Marquette   1674–75

Marquette's brief visit to the Illinois Indians in 1673 had convinced him that they would receive Christianity more readily than did the northern tribes. He was elated when in 1674 he gained permission to found a mission to the Illinois. On October 25, 1674, the 38-year-old Marquette and two French companions embarked from the Jesuit mission at Green Bay, bound for the Illinois Country. As winter came on, Father Marquette's health failed rapidly. In his diary he wrote fragmentary notes describing the voyage along the west coast of Lake Michigan.

October 26. On passing the village of the Potawatomies [on Green Bay] we learn that five canoes of Potawatomies and four of Illinois have embarked for the Kaskaskia [Illinois].

27. We are delayed in the morning by rain, but fine calm weather in the afternoon allows us to join the savages at Sturgeon Bay.

28. We reach the portage [between Sturgeon Bay and Lake Michigan]. A canoe that has gone ahead prevents us from killing game. Stormy weather gives us much trouble. After rain and thunder, snow falls.

29. We continue to carry our packs. The portage covers three miles, and is very difficult in many places. In the evening the Illinois

Missionary, by Frederic Remington

join us and ask us not to leave them. They say we may need them. We promise them this.

30. The Illinois women carry the rest of our things across the portage in the morning. We are delayed by wind.

31. We start, with tolerably fair weather, and sleep at a small river.

November 1. We come for the night to a river [Kewaunee River] that one follows to go to the Potawatomies. An Illinois arrives at night with a deer on his back.

2. We travel all day in very fine weather. We kill two racoons, which are almost nothing but fat.

3. While I am ashore, walking on fine sand, I come to a river that I cannot cross [Manitowoc River]. Our canoe enters the river to take me on board, but we cannot go back out, because of the waves.

5. We get out of the river at noon, and soon find the Illinois giving a feast to a wolfskin. I seize the opportunity to instruct them in Christianity.

23. Embarking at noon, we have trouble in reaching a river [probably Pike River of Kenosha County, Wisconsin]. Here we are delayed for three days, during which time Pierre kills a deer, three geese and three turkeys, which are very good. The others go out onto the prairies, where they discover Mascoutens in eight or nine lodges, who have separated from their people to obtain food. The Mascoutens' lodges are wretched. They eat or starve, according to the places they happen to be. Enduring fatigues almost impossible for Frenchmen, they travel throughout the winter over very bad trails, in a country abounding with streams, small lakes and swamps. Here the cold begins. More than a foot of snow covers the ground and remains. I have an attack of diarrhea.

27. We have some trouble in getting out of the river. We notice there are great shoals out in the lake, over which the waves break continually. After proceeding about eight miles, we find the Illinois, who have killed some buffalo. We are delayed by wind from the land, by heavy waves from the lake, and by cold.

61

December 3. After saying holy mass, we embark, but are compelled to make for a point of land, on account of floating masses of ice.

4. We start with a favoring wind, and reach the river of the portage [Chicago River] which is frozen over. There is more snow here than elsewhere, and more tracks of animals and turkeys.

12. During our stay at the mouth of the river [the site of downtown Chicago], Pierre and Jacques kill three buffalo and four deer, one of which runs some distance with its heart split in two. We content ourselves with killing three or four of the many turkeys that come near our cabin. They are almost dying of hunger. Jacques brings in a prairie chicken, like the partridges in France, except this one has no feathers on the sides of the neck. We begin to haul our baggage to approach the portage.

14. We decide to winter near the portage, five miles up the river, since my illness will not allow me any more fatigue. [This portage, in what is now southwest Chicago, linked the Chicago River with the Des Plaines River.] Several Illinois pass by, carrying furs. We give them a buffalo and a deer that Jacques had killed.

15. The Illinois who accompanied us, now leave us to join their people. They trade us three fine robes of buffalo skin for a cubit of tobacco. The robes are very useful to us during the winter. I have never seen Indians more eager for French tobacco. After the 14th, my disease turns into a bloody flux.

30. Jacques returns from the Illinois village just 16 miles from here. There the Illinois are suffering from hunger, because the cold and snow prevent them from hunting.

January 16, 1675. I send Jacques to tell the Illinois that my illness prevents me from going to them, and that I will have trouble going to them in the spring, should my illness continue.

24. Jacques returns with a sack of corn and other delicacies. He also brings the tongues and flesh of two buffalo. All animals feel the bad weather.

26. Three Illinois bring us two sacks of corn, dried meat, pumpkins and twelve beaver skins. They make a mat for me and ask me for gun powder. I refuse them the gun powder, saying that I do not

want them to start war with the Miamis. To reward them for their trouble, I give them a hatchet, two knives, three clasp-knives, ten brasses of glass beads and two double mirrors. I tell them that I will try to go to their village, but for only a few days if my illness continues. They tell me to take courage, and to remain to die in their country.

February 9. My bloody flux has left me, since we addressed the Blessed Virgin Immaculate and began a novena to ask God to restore my health. I begin to feel much better and I regain my strength. All that remains is a weakness in my stomach.

March 30. A north wind delayed the thaw until the 25th of March, when the thaw finally set in with a south wind. On the very next day game began to appear. We killed nearly 30 wild pigeons. On the 28th the ice broke up, then jammed on the river above us. On the 29th the water rose so fast we barely had time to decamp, placing our goods in trees and trying to sleep on a hillock. The water gained on us all night. Because the water was already rising, we embarked to continue our voyage.

31. The water has risen 12 feet, and only the very high lands are not flooded. Geese and ducks pass continually. We content ourselves with shooting seven. Drifting ice keeps us from embarking.

April 6. Two lakes over which we pass are full of herons, geese, ducks, and other game unknown to us. The rapids are quite dangerous in places.

> *Marquette's journal entry of April 6th was his last. His story is continued below by Father Claude Dablon, superior of the Jesuit missions in the Upper Country.*

On at last arriving at the Illinois village, [near the site of Utica, Illinois], Father Marquette was received as an angel from Heaven. On April 11th he addressed the whole village, preaching to them of Jesus Christ. This was on the very eve of the day when Jesus died on the cross for them. On Easter Sunday Father Marquette celebrated the holy mysteries for a second time. But soon his illness obliged him to leave the Illinois, who begged him to return to them as soon as possible.

63

He continued his journey to Lake Michigan, where he was obliged to follow the eastern coast. His strength was failing so rapidly that his two companions despaired of bringing him alive to the end of his journey. He became so feeble and exhausted that he had to be handled and carried about like a child.

The evening before his death, he joyously told his companions that he would die on the morrow. The next day, as they made their way on the lake, he saw a hill near a river [Pere Marquette River at the site of Ludington, Michigan]. He told them that this spot would be the place of his last repose. They brought him to land, lighted a little fire, and prepared for him a wretched little hut. They were so stricken with grief, they hardly knew what they were doing. They drew near to him, he embraced them, and they burst into tears at his feet. Removing his crucifix from around his neck, he asked one of his companions to hold it before his eyes. Sensing that he had but a short time to live, he made a last effort, clasped his hands, and with a steady gaze upon his crucifix, he gave thanks to God for the great favor of dying in the Society of Jesus as a missionary of Jesus Christ, in a wretched cabin, in the midst of the forests. He then asked his companions to repeat the names of Jesus and Mary when they see him about to die. At the moment they believed him to be near his end, one of them called aloud, "Jesus, Mary!" The dying man repeated the words distinctly, and as if something presented itself to him, he suddenly raised his eyes above his crucifix. Beaming and all aglow, he died without struggle, so gently that death appeared to be a gentle sleep.

FRESHWATER SEAS

Father Louis Hennepin   1679

*No Frenchman held a grander dream of empire than
did Robert Cavelier de la Salle. In the 1670's, while
most French Canadians concentrated on the fur trade,
La Salle sought to push the boundaries of New France
far westward into the remote wilderness. He envisioned
a French empire encompassing the vast heartland of
the continent drained by the Mississippi River. The
young La Salle pursued his grand plan with single-
minded fervor. His first step was to build a ship on
Lake Erie, the first ever to sail on the Upper Great Lakes.
La Salle's expedition of 1679–80 was described by
Father Louis Hennepin, a Franciscan priest who accompanied the voyage.*

In 1678 the Sieur de La Salle went to France to ask
permission to discover the mouth of the great River
Meschasipi [Mississippi]. His object was to discover
rich, fertile and temperate countries, where the trade in skins and
wool of the buffalo might support powerful colonies. La Salle wished
to build ships at the mouth of the Mississippi, to transport buffalo
skins. In view of the great expense, he was granted the exclusive
trade in buffalo skins.

La Salle returned to Canada in July of 1678 with a company of
30, including the Sieurs la Motte and Tonty, myself, a pilot, sailors,

65

shipwrights, carpenters, a blacksmith and others. We carried anchors, rigging for ships, weapons and supplies.

Ten miles from Lake Frontenac [Lake Ontario], there is an incredible waterfall [Niagara Falls] that thunders continually, plunging more than 300 feet into waters that foam and boil in a fearful manner. La Salle was compelled to build his ship five miles above this great fall. From there one may sail in a large ship from Lake Ontario to the end of Lake Dauphin [Lake Michigan], over lakes which may be called freshwater seas. They all abound in fish and are easily navigated, except in winter when high winds prevail.

Most of the Iroquois Indians who lived near this shipyard had gone to war beyond Lake Conty [Lake Erie], but those remaining came often to show their displeasure. One of them, pretending to be drunk, wanted to kill the blacksmith, but the French forced him to leave. Later a woman warned us that the Iroquois wanted to set fire to our ship while it was on the stocks, so we kept strict watch. These frequent alarms, the fear of running out of food, and the refusal of the Iroquois to sell us Indian corn astonished our carpenters. They wanted to leave, and one tried to go over to the Dutch at New York.

In a short time we launched our ship, although not entirely finished, to protect it from the threat of fire. It was blessed and named the Griffin. We fired three salutes with our cannon, sang the Te Deum in thanksgiving, and shouted, "Vive le Roy." [Long live the King]. The Iroquois stood wondering at this ceremony, and they shared in our rejoicing. A glass of brandy was given to all, Iroquois as well as French.

So we left our bark cabins to sleep in the ship on the water, safe from the insults of the Indians. The Iroquois who returned from war were astonished. They said the French were "spirits." They could not understand how we could build so large a wooden canoe in so short a time. This ship, a mobile fort of about 45 tons, would make the Indians tremble across 1,300 miles of country.

We set sail the 7th of August, 1679, steering west by south. After chanting the Te Deum, we fired all our cannon in the presence of several Iroquois, who later described the size of our ship to the Dutch.

66

French ships circa 1680, by Vander Gucht

Our voyage was so fortunate that on the morning of the 10th day we entered the Strait of Detroit, where Lake Orleans [Lake Huron] empties into Lake Erie. This strait is two miles wide, except in the middle, where it expands and forms a circular lake which we named Lake St. Clare. The country on both sides of this beautiful strait is adorned with fine, open plains, where you can see numbers of deer, bear (not fierce, and very good to eat), all kinds of game, waterfowl, and swans in abundance. The rest of the strait is covered with forests—walnuts, chestnuts, plum and apple trees—and wild vines loaded with grapes from which we made wine.

At the entrance to Lake Huron we encountered a furious current, caused by a violent north wind which had been blowing for some time. Though aided by a strong south wind, we could not stem the current under sail, so we landed 12 men who towed the ship from the beach. We entered Lake Huron, and for the second time we chanted a Te Deum in thanksgiving.

At midnight of the 25th we were forced to head north past a great point that jutted into the lake. We had scarcely doubled this point when we were surprised by a furious gale which forced us to ply windward with mainsail and foresail, then lie to until daylight. The next day the violence of the wind forced us to lower the top-masts, fasten the yards and clew, and remain broadside to shore. The waves ran high, but we could find no anchorage or shelter. At this crisis, La Salle entered the cabin and, quite disheartened, told us that he now commended his enterprise to God. All made an act of contrition except our pilot, whom I was never able to win over to our faith.

That night the wind fell a little as we lay to, and we drifted only three or four miles.

Soon we arrived at Missilimackinac [Mackinac], where Lake Michigan empties into Lake Huron. Indians living at Mackinac were amazed to see a ship in their country, and the sound of our cannon caused extraordinary alarm. We went to the Ottawas to say mass. There La Salle, dressed in his scarlet cloak trimmed with gold lace, ordered the weapons stacked outside the little chapel, under guard. As we came out, we spied the Griffin, riding at anchor in the bay.

With pleasure we gazed at this large, well-equipped ship, amid 100 Indian canoes.

Mackinac and Sault St. Marie, where Lake Conde [Lake Superior] empties into Lake Huron, are the two most important passages for all the Indians of the west and north, who carry their furs to Montreal every year to trade.

On the 2nd of September we left Mackinac and entered Lake Michigan. We arrived at an island [Washington Island] at the entrance to La Baye des Puants [Green Bay]. The island is inhabited by Potawatomies. The chief of this nation had his warriors dance the peace pipe to La Salle.

Against our advice, La Salle decided to send his ship back to Niagara with a cargo of furs, there to take on more supplies and return to Mackinac for directions. The crew of the Griffin set sail on the 18th of September, with a favorable west wind, bidding adieu by firing a single cannon.

We never would learn what course the ship took, but there is no doubt that she soon perished. We later learned from Indians that the ship had anchored in the north of Lake Huron, but the pilot, against the advice of Indians who said there was a great storm in the middle of the lake, decided to continue his voyage. (He did not know the force of the wind, because of the sheltered position of his anchorage.) He scarcely sailed a mile from the coast when the Indians saw the ship tossing, unable to resist the tempest. In a short time they lost sight of her, and they think she foundered or was driven aground. The loss of the Griffin cost La Salle more than 40,000 livres worth of goods, tools and furs, men, and the rigging he had imported from France and had carried from Montreal in bark canoes. We did not learn of the shipwreck until the next year.

As for our party, we set out on September 19th, fourteen men in four canoes. I steered the smallest, loaded with 500 pounds of goods and a carpenter newly arrived from France, who did not know how to avoid the waves. In rough weather I had great trouble managing this little craft. Our four bark canoes were loaded with a forge and all accessories, plus weapons, merchandise and tools. We took our course southerly toward the mainland, but in the middle of this

69

traverse, amid the most beautiful calm in the world, a storm came up that threatened our lives. We completed this passage in the night, calling out to one another. We reached a little sandy bay and stayed five days, waiting for the lake to grow calm. The wind lasted four days, with a fury like the greatest tempests of the ocean. During this stay, our Indian hunter killed only a single porcupine, which seasoned our squashes and Indian corn.

On October 1st we arrived near another village of Potawatomies [somewhere on the western shore of Lake Michigan]. They flocked to the lake shore to haul us in from the great waves, but La Salle, fearing his men would desert, pushed on and landed eight miles beyond the village. We were not familiar with that village, so La Salle ordered the weapons readied, and posted himself on a hill that could be defended by a small force. He then sent three men to buy food at the village, under the protection of the pipe of peace which the Potawatomies of the island had given him. This was a large pipe. The head was of polished, red stone, and the stem was a stout cane adorned with colored feathers, tresses of braided women's hair and two bird wings. A pipe of this kind is a sure passport among all allies of those who have given it. They believe great harm would befall them if they violated the faith of the pipe. Their most important ceremonies and all their ventures in war and peace are sealed by smoking the pipe. The three Frenchmen arrived with this safeguard at the small Potawatomi village, but found no one there. The Indians, seeing that we had not landed, had taken fright and abandoned their village. The Frenchmen took what corn they could carry and left merchandise in its place.

Meanwhile, 20 of the Potawatomies approached us, armed with guns, axes, bows, arrows and clubs. La Salle advanced to confront them with four of his men, armed with guns, pistols and sabres. He asked them what they wished, and seeing that they were perplexed, he told them to come on. He made them sit at the foot of the hill on which we made camp. There we could watch their movements. Soon our three Frenchmen returned and the Indians saw the pipe they carried. The Indians shouted a great cry of joy and began to dance. They were not angry about the corn, but sent to the village

70

to bring us more. La Salle thanked them with a gift of axes, knives and beads.

We set out on October 2nd and canoed for four days along the shore, which was bordered by cliffs, with scarcely a place to land. Every evening we were forced to climb to the summit, carrying our canoes and cargoes, to keep them from the waves. We ate the Indian corn sparingly, as our food gradually failed us. All this time we were obliged to keep on toward a good county, and to paddle with all our strength for whole days. One day during this scarcity, we saw several crows and eagles on the lake shore. Zealously paddling toward those birds, we found a very fat deer, killed by wolves and half eaten. We restored ourselves with the flesh of this animal.

As our little fleet advanced toward the south, we found the country always finer and more temperate. On the 16th of October we began to see a great abundance of game. Our Indian killed deer, and our Frenchmen killed very fat waterfowl.

At last, on the 28th of October, we reached the southern end of Lake Michigan. There we found ripe grapes, large as damson plums. To get the grapes we had to cut down the trees on which the vines grew. We made wine for mass, and we ate grapes to make the meat palatable, for we had no bread.

At this place we noticed fresh footprints of men, and La Salle was forced to keep his men on guard and silent. All our men obeyed for a time; but one, seeing a bear, fired his gun at it. The shot killed the bear and sent it rolling from the top of the cliff to the foot of our cabins. This shot announced us to 120 Indians of the nation of the Outagamies [Foxes]. La Salle was very uneasy. To prevent a surprise, he posted a sentry near the canoes and the goods.

This did not prevent 30 Foxes, under the cover of rain that fell in torrents, from gliding by night, with their usual stealth, along the hill to our canoes. Lying on their bellies, side by side, they stole the coat of La Salle's servant and the goods under it, passing them from hand to hand. Our sentry, hearing noise, roused us, and our men ran to arms. Their chief then called out that he was a friend. We replied that men do not come in that fashion by night, except to steal or kill those not on their guard. He answered that the shot they heard

71

had made them think we were a party of Iroquois, their enemies, and they had advanced to kill them. We pretended to credit these reasons, and we let them retire.

After they left, our ship's carpenters discovered that we had been robbed. We knew the Indians would try again every night if we ignored this, so we decided to insist on redress. La Salle, at the head of our men, took as prisoner one of the most important Indians, and sent word to the Foxes that he would kill their comrade if they did not bring back all they had stolen.

The savages were unable to return the goods whole, because they had cut the servant's red coat in pieces. They resolved to rescue their comrade by force. The next morning they advanced, arms in hand, to begin the attack. The peninsula where we had camped was separated from the wood by a sandy plain two gun shots wide, and near the wood were several mounds. La Salle occupied the highest, commanding five men who carried their blankets rolled around the left arm to shield themselves from arrows.

I came out of our cabin to see what figure our men made under arms, and to encourage two of the youngest whom I saw grow pale. I then approached the oldest Indians. They saw I was unarmed and they assumed that I would part the combatants and act as mediator.

The bold actions of a few Frenchmen against 125 Indians so impressed the savages that two of the old men near me presented a peace pipe. We assured them that they could advance without fear. They promised to return to us what was whole, and to pay for the rest. Thus peace was restored.

The next day was spent in dances, feasts and speeches. The head chief, turning toward the Franciscan fathers, said, "See the gray gowns. They go barefoot like us. They despise the beaver robes that we seek to give them. They have no weapons to kill us. They flatter and caress our little children, and give them beads. You who are the chief [La Salle], let one of the gray gowns stay with us. You who are the master, stay also with us. Do not go to the Illinois, for we know that they wish to massacre all the French. You cannot resist that numerous nation."

This alarmed all our Frenchmen and disturbed La Salle, who had heard the same thing from other Indians on our route. Nevertheless, La Salle understood the jealousy of the Indians, who knew the courage of the Illinois and who feared that the Illinois might become even more haughty when they acquired the use of French firearms. La Salle thanked the Foxes for their advice, but answered that the French—who are spirits—do not fear the Illinois, and would bring them to reason by friendship or by force.

On the 1st of November we arrived at the rendezvous we had arranged with 20 other Frenchmen who we expected to come along the east coast of Lake Michigan. The rendezvous was at the mouth of the River of the Miamis [St. Joseph River], which flows from the south and empties into Lake Michigan [at the site of Benton Harbor, Michigan]. We were surprised to find no one there.

November was spent building a fort, during which time we ate nothing but bear meat. Many bears were attracted to this place by the grapes growing there. Our workers were discouraged by the rigorous setting in of winter, seeing La Salle unmanned by the fear of losing his ship, and they were utterly annoyed at the delay of the other men. Our mechanics worked only reluctantly. They stormed against the fat bear meat and at being forbidden to go kill deer. Their aim tended to desertion.

We sounded the mouth of the river and discovered a sand bar there. To aid the entrance of our ship, in case it arrived, we marked the channel by two tall poles with bear skin pendants.

On the 20th of November the Sieur de Tonty arrived with two canoes loaded with deer meat. This revived a little the sagging spirits of our workmen. Tonty reported that our ship had not touched at Mackinac, and he had heard no word of it from the Indians, who had come from all sides of the lakes. La Salle feared, with reason, that his ship had perished.

PRAIRIE

Father Louis Hennepin   1679–80

As the winter of 1680 set in, La Salle's situation was grim. He feared that his ship, with a rich cargo of furs, was lost. He gave up hope that more supplies would arrive. His men were hungry and mutinous. His camp, on the south shore of Lake Michigan, was hundreds of miles from the nearest French outpost. Yet he ordered his men to push onward, toward the Illinois Country.

We embarked on the 3rd of December with 32 men in eight canoes, and we ascended the River of the Miamis [St. Joseph River of northwest Indiana]. La Salle had gone to explore by land, and when he did not return, we did not know what course to pursue. The next afternoon we saw him at a distance, his hands and face all black from the fire he had lit during the night. Hanging at his belt, he had two animals [opossums], the size of muskrats, which had beautiful fur like ermine. These animals often hang by the tail from a branch. He had killed them with a stick, without them fleeing. Our canoemen feasted on them.

Father Gabriel and I begged La Salle not to leave our party again, because the whole success of our voyage depended on his leadership.

The next day we found the portage at the edge of a great plain [the site of South Bend, Indiana]. There we saw buffalo horns and carcasses, and some canoes the Indians had made from buffalo skin to cross the river with their loads of meat. On the western edge of this plain is a village of Miamis, Mascouten and Wea living together.

74

The River Seignelay [Kankakee River], which flows toward the Illinois nation, has its source in this plain in the middle of much boggy land. It is navigable by canoe to within a hundred paces of its source. It takes its course through vast marshes, and winds about so, that after canoeing on it for a whole day, we sometimes found we had not advanced more than five miles in a straight line. As far as the eye could reach, nothing was seen but marshes full of reeds and alders. For more than 100 miles we found no place to camp except for hummocks of frozen earth, on which we lit our fire and slept. Our food ran out and we found no game after passing those marshes, as we had hoped. We saw only great open prairies. The tall grass was dry in this season, and had been burned by the Miamis while hunting buffalo. We saw bones, horns and skulls of buffaloes on all sides. We tried to kill deer, but for more than 150 miles our hunters killed only a small deer, a lean buck, swans, and two wild geese—these to feed 32 men. If our men had found a chance, they would have abandoned us to strike inland and join the Indians. We could detect the Indians by flames on the prairies, which they set to hunt the buffalo more easily.

The Miamis hunt the buffalo toward the end of autumn. When they find a herd, they gather in great numbers and set fire to the tall grass around the herd, leaving only a small passage where they take post with their bows and arrows. The buffalo, fleeing the fire, are forced to pass near the Indians, who sometimes kill as many as 120 in a day. The Indian hunters, triumphant at the massacre of so many animals, notify their women, who at once go to bring in the meat. Some women carry 300 pounds on their backs, and throw their children on top of the load, which does not seem to burden them any more than a sword burdens a soldier. The Indians distribute their kill according to the needs of each family. The women spin the wool of the buffalo to make bags for carrying the meat, which is sometimes dried in the sun. They have no salt, but they dry the meat so well that four months after it is dressed, one can eat it and think it was just killed.

The skin of a buffalo weighs from 100 to 120 pounds. The Indians cut away the heaviest parts, the back and neck, and use the

75

Buffalo chase in winter, by George Catlin

thinnest part from the belly, dressing it very neatly. They use animal brains to render it as supple as our chamois skins dressed with oil. They paint it different colors, trim it with red and white porcupine quills, and make fine robes of it for their festivals. These robes, full of curly wool, have a pleasing appearance. In winter the Indians use buffalo skins as blankets.

When the Indians kill buffalo cows, the little calves follow the hunters and lick their fingers. The Indians sometimes take a calf to their children, who play with it, then strike it on the head to be eaten. They save the hooves of little calves, dry them, and tie them to sticks. They rattle these sticks like tambourines at their dances.

The meat of the buffalo is succulent. They are fat in the autumn, because all summer they have been up to their necks in grass. This vast country, so full of prairies, seems to be the element and the country of the buffalo. There are also groves of trees where these animals go to ruminate and escape the heat of the sun. The cows sometimes go to islands in the rivers to protect their young calves from wolves. Even when the calves can run, the wolves do not venture to attack, because the cows would kill them.

The buffalo herds change country according to the season. When they approach the northern lands and feel the beginning of winter, they pass to the south. They follow one another in a herd that sometimes extends for three miles. Their path is beaten like our great roads of Europe, and no grass grows on it. When they are surprised by winter and cannot reach the warm country, they turn up the snow to crop the grass beneath.

The Indians have the foresight not to drive the buffalo from their country. They chase only those wounded by arrows, and do not pursue the others, so as not to frighten them too much. The Indians of this vast continent cannot exterminate the buffalo, for these beasts multiply in great numbers. Buffaloes are very large, but their great bulk does not hinder them from moving very fast. Few Indians can run them down, and the bulls often kill Indians who have wounded them.

Many other animals are found on these vast plains. Deer, beaver and otter are common. Geese, swans, turtles, parrots, prairie chickens and many other birds swarm here. Fish are abundant and the soil is fertile. There are boundless prairies interspersed with forests of tall trees, ideal for ship building. The country is watered by countless lakes, rivers and streams, most of them navigable.

We continued our route down the Illinois River for the rest of December, and during that time we killed only some water fowl, because the Indians had set fire to all the prairies on our route, and the deer had taken flight. We survived only by the providence of God. Once when we had nothing more to eat, we found an enormous buffalo mired at the bank of the river. Twelve of our men had trouble dragging it to solid ground.

At the end of December we arrived at a village of the Illinois Indians on the right bank of the river [near the site of Utica, Illinois]. It contained 460 lodges built like long arbors, covered with double mats of flat reeds, so well sewn that they kept out wind, rain and snow. Each lodge had four or five fires, and each fire had one or two families. However, we found the village empty. All the Illinois had gone to different places for the winter hunt, as was their custom. This was a great problem for us, because our food had run out, but we dared not take the Indian corn, which the Illinois hide in trenches under ground. They need this corn for planting and survival until the next harvest. This stock is most precious to them, and to take it would be a great offense. Nevertheless, La Salle decided to take 20 bushels, hoping to appease the Illinois in some way.

On January 4th, while crossing a small lake formed by the river [Lake Peoria], we saw smoke from lodges. The next morning we saw dug-out canoes on both sides of the river and about 80 lodges of the Illinois. We gave a cry to ask whether they wished peace or war, because it was important to show resolution at the outset. We approached in eight canoes abreast, drifting with the current, all our men with arms in hand. Their old men, women and children took flight. Their warriors ran to their weapons, but in great confusion. Our canoes touched land, and La Salle was the first to leap ashore. Here we halted, to give the Illinois time to regain confidence. A chief on the opposite side of the river saw that we refrained from firing, and he shouted to prevent his warriors from shooting arrows. Two of the warriors who understood the situation came down the hill to present the peace pipe.

After dances and feasts which lasted the day, we told them that we Franciscan priests had not come to gather beaver, but to give them knowledge of the great Master of Life. They shouted their approval and rubbed our legs and feet with bear oil and buffalo grease, to relieve our fatigue. They put the first three morsels of meat in our mouths, with extraordinary gestures of friendship.

La Salle then gave them tobacco and axes, and admitted to them that he had taken their corn. He said he would trade axes and other things for it, but if they could not spare the corn, they were free to take it back. He added that if they could not supply the food his men needed, he would go to the neighboring Osages, who would furnish corn in exchange for a blacksmith who could fix their axes. They accepted La Salle's payment with great joy, and even gave us more corn. They begged us to settle among them. We answered that we would, and that we intended to bring other Frenchmen who would furnish all the goods they needed. We said we must first build a great wooden canoe to sail down to the sea. We asked them whether their river was navigable to the sea. They told us about the River Mississippi, describing its width and beauty. They assured us that the navigation was free and easy, and that there were no Europeans near its mouth. They added that Indian prisoners whom they had captured in the direction of the sea said they had seen ships far out which made sounds that resembled thunder.

Our men spent the winter building a fort that we called Crevecœur [near the site of Peoria, Illinois], and making planks for a ship. But we had no rigging, sails or iron for a new ship, and we heard no tidings of the ship we had left on Lake Michigan. With summer approaching, La Salle worried that if he waited uselessly for some months, our enterprise would be delayed a full year or more. He decided to go on foot with three other French to Fort Frontenac itself [on the northeast coast of Lake Ontario], a distance of more than 1,300 miles. There he would put his affairs in order and have the needed supplies forwarded. La Salle left Tonty as commander at Fort Crevecœur, with carpenters and a blacksmith to build a ship, and soldiers with arms in case they were attacked by the Iroquois.

La Salle then asked me to go with two Frenchmen into unexplored countries, where every moment our lives would be in great danger.

CAPTURED BY THE SIOUX

Father Louis Hennepin   1680

Following La Salle's orders, Father Hennepin and two French companions set off by canoe, first down the Illinois River, then up the Mississippi. Their destination was the headwaters of the Mississippi, the country of the "Nadouessiou," the unexplored land of an unknown people. As the three men canoed up the broad Mississippi, Father Hennepin prayed that they would survive.

We begged of God to meet those Indians by day, for by night they kill people as enemies, and rob them of axes or knives, which they value more than we value gold or silver. Our prayers were answered on April 11th, 1680, when we suddenly saw 33 bark canoes, manned by 120 Nadouessious [Sioux]. They were coming down the river with extraordinary speed, to make war on the Miamis, Illinois and Maroa. From a distance they shot arrows at us, but as they drew near our canoe, the old men saw the peace pipe in my hands and prevented the young men from killing us. Some of those brutal men leapt into the water. One wrenched the peace pipe from my hands. They made us cross the river, paddling ahead of them. They made great cries, all shouted together, filling us with terror.

After landing, the eldest among them uttered the words, "Miamiha, Miamiha." I understood them to be asking about the Miamis.

81

We did not speak their language, so we drew signs on the sand with a stick to show them that their enemies, the Miamis, had fled across the Mississippi River to join the Illinois. When the Sioux knew themselves to be discovered and unable to surprise their enemies, three or four old men, laying their hands on my head, wept in a mournful tone. I wiped away their tears with my wretched handkerchief, but they refused to smoke our peace pipe.

They soon met in council to decide what to do with us. The two chiefs of the war party showed us, by signs, that the warriors wished to tomahawk us. This compelled me to go to the war chiefs with one of my men, leaving the other with our property. I threw into their midst six axes, fifteen knives and six fathom of black tobacco. I then bowed down my head and showed them with an axe that they might kill us, if they thought proper. The gift appeased many of them, who gave us beaver meat, putting the first three morsels in our mouths, according to their custom, and blowing on the meat that was too hot.

Nevertheless, they gave us back our peace pipe, so we spent the night in fear. My two companions resolved to sell their lives dearly and to resist if attacked. Their arms and swords were ready. As for me, I decided to let myself be killed without resistance, to announce to the Sioux a God who had been cruelly crucified, without aversion to those who put him to death. We took turns keeping watch, so as not to be surprised.

In the morning a young chief named Narrhetoba—his face and body smeared with paint—asked for our peace pipe, filled it with his tobacco, made his warriors smoke first, then offered it to those who plotted our ruin. He made us understand that they would turn back, and that we must go with them to their country.

The outrages done us by these Indians were incredible. Our captors were from different villages, and they had different opinions regarding us. We slept every night near the young chief who had asked for our peace pipe, putting ourselves under his protection. Jealousy arose among the Indians. A chief named Aquipaguetin, who had a son killed by the Miamis, saw that he could not avenge his son's death on the Miami nation, so he turned all his rage on us.

82

Through almost every night he wept for his lost son, trying to oblige his comrades to kill us and seize our goods. But those who wanted European goods wished to save us, to attract other Frenchmen to their country, and to obtain iron, extremely precious in their eyes. The words *mauza ouackange* mean "iron that has understanding," and so these nations call a gun, which can break a man's bones, while their arrows only glance through the flesh.

When the weather was good we slept on the ground without shelter. This gave us time to contemplate the stars and moon. Often the young warriors danced the war pipe till midnight; yet despite their yelling, their fatigue from the day, and their watch by night, the old men all awoke at daybreak for fear of being surprised by their enemies. As soon as dawn appeared, one of them gave the cry, and in an instant all the warriors entered their bark canoes. Some went around the islands in the river to kill beasts. The most alert went by land to scout for the fires of an enemy.

The enemies of the Sioux have only dug-out, wooden canoes, which cannot go as fast as the lighter bark canoes of the Sioux. Only northern tribes have birch trees to make bark canoes, which wonderfully help them in going from lake to lake and by rivers, to attack their enemies. Even when discovered by their enemies, they are safe if they can get into their bark canoes, for their enemies cannot pursue them fast enough.

During 19 days of painful navigation up the Mississippi River, my greatest trouble was in saying my prayers before the Indians. Seeing me move my lips, they fiercely said, "*Ouakanche.*" They thought that the book I was reading was a spirit. To get them used to it, I chanted the litany of the Blessed Virgin with my book open. They thought the prayer book was a spirit which taught me to sing for their pleasure, for those people are naturally fond of singing.

One day we stopped about noon at a large prairie. Having killed a very fat bear, Aquipaguetin gave a feast to the great chief. After the feast the warriors danced, their faces and bodies marked with colors, each in the figure of a different animal. Some had their hair short and full of bear oil, sprinkled with bird's down. Others wore white and red feathers. All danced with their arms akimbo and struck

83

Sioux braves dance, by George Catlin

the ground so stoutly as to leave footprints. The father, in a doleful voice broken with sighs and sobs, his whole body bathed in tears, sometimes came to me and put his hands on my head, doing the same to my two Frenchmen. As far as we could tell, this whole ceremony tended to our destruction. This Indian had often aimed at our lives, but the other chiefs protected us. We slept that night at the point of the Lake of Tears [Lake Pepin], which we named for the tears this chief and his sons shed all night long.

Those Indians sometimes sent their swiftest warriors by land to chase the buffalo toward the water. As the animals crossed the river, the Indians sometimes killed 40 or 50, merely to take the tongue and most delicate morsels.

On the 19th day of our navigation we landed in a bay, 12 miles below the Falls of St. Anthony [south of the site of St. Paul]. They gave each of us to the head of a family—in place of a son who had been killed in war—and they broke our canoe to pieces, for fear we would escape to their enemies. Although we could easily have reached their country by water, they forced us to march from daybreak to two hours after nightfall for 150 miles, and to swim across many rivers. On leaving the cold water, I could scarcely stand. We ate a few pieces of meat just once a day. I was so weak that I often lay down to die, rather than follow those Indians, who marched with a speed that surpasses the strength of Europeans. To force us onward, they often set fire to the grass of the prairies, so we had to advance or burn.

As we approached their village [at Mille Lacs Lake], the savages took all the articles of my portable chapel except the chalice, which they dared not touch. Seeing its glittering silver gilt, they closed their eyes, saying it was a spirit which would kill them. One of the principal chiefs gave us his peace pipe to smoke, and accepted ours. He gave us wild rice seasoned with whortleberries, the best meal we had had in seven or eight days. After this feast, the head of each family who adopted us led each of us to his village.

The day after our arrival, Aquipaguetin, who was head of a large family, covered me with a robe made of ten beaver skins, trimmed with porcupine quills. He told five or six of his wives that they should consider me one of their children. Seeing that I could not rise from the ground without help, he had a sweat lodge made. It was covered with buffalo skins, with red-hot stones inside. He made me enter naked with four Indians. He made me a sign to do like the others before beginning to sweat, but I merely concealed my nakedness with a handkerchief. As soon as the Indians had breathed out quite violently several times, he began to sing in a thundering voice. The others seconded him, all putting their hands on me and rubbing me, as they wept bitterly. I began to faint. When I came out, I could hardly lift my gown to put it on. Yet after he had made me sweat three times a week, I felt as strong as ever.

I often spent sad hours among those savages. They gave me only a little wild rice, and smoked fish eggs five or six times a week. I would have been satisfied if they had fed me like one of their children, but they ate secretly at night, unknown to me. Although the women were more kind and compassionate than the men, they gave what little fish they had to their children, regarding me as a slave captured by their warriors in the enemy's country. Reasonably, they preferred their children's lives to mine.

Aquipaguetin took me with his wives and children to a neighboring island, there to sow tobacco seeds and vegetable seeds that I had brought, which he prized extremely.

As soon as I learned the word "*taketchiabihen*," which in their language means "What do you call that?", I began to talk with them. They often put questions to me. They wondered why I had to look at my paper to answer them. "That white thing," they said, "must be a spirit which tells Father Louis all we say." The chiefs often made me write on paper the parts of the human body. They were amused when I would not write certain indelicate words, at which they do not blush. The Indians often asked how many wives and children I had. They were surprised at my answer. I said that a man among us could have only one wife until death, and that as for me, I had promised the Master of Life to live as they saw me, and to teach them to live like the French. I told them that the great Master of Life once had sent fire down from heaven to destroy a nation given to enormous crimes, like those they committed. But those gross people turned all I said to ridicule. They asked, "How could your two men get wives? Our women would not live with them, for they have hair all over their faces."

They knew I carried a compass in my sleeve. Seeing that I could turn the needle with a key, and understanding that we Europeans went all over the globe guided by this instrument, they believed that we were spirits, able to do things beyond their reach. They never dared to touch my iron pot, which had three lion-claw feet.

Some of the old men often came to weep over my head, one saying in a sighing voice, "My grandson, I feel sorry to see you are not eating, and to learn how badly our warriors treated you on the way. They are young braves without sense, who have robbed you of all you had and who would have killed you. If you want buffalo or beaver robes, we will wipe away your tears. But you will take nothing of what we offer you."

Ouasicoude, or Pierced Pine, the greatest of all chiefs, was indignant at those who had treated us badly. In open council he said those who had robbed us were like hungry dogs that stealthily snatch a bit of meat from the bark dish and then run.

In the beginning of July, 1680, all the nations assembled, and the chiefs determined the places for hunting buffalo. They dispersed in several bands, so as not to starve each other. Our band of 130 families and 250 warriors was to descend southward by canoe with the great chief Ouasicoude. As they departed, the Indians would not give me a place in one of their small canoes, for they had only old canoes. I stood on the bank of the River of the Sioux [Rum River] and stretched out my hand to the canoes as they passed rapidly, one after another. My two Frenchmen, Michel Accault and Picard du Gay, had a canoe for themselves, but would not take me in. Michel Accault said he had taken me long enough to satisfy him. I was deeply hurt by this answer, seeing myself abandoned by Christians. But God, who has never abandoned me, prompted two Indians to take me into their small, leaky canoe, where I had no other job than to bail water with a bark platter. This canoe could be called a coffin, because of its lightness and fragility. It weighed less than 50 pounds, and the least motion would have upset it.

87

Falls of St. Anthony, by Seth Eastman

Four days later we halted on a hill opposite the mouth of the Rum River [near the present site of Anoka, Minnesota]. Here we asked the Indians to let us proceed down the Mississippi River to the mouth of the River Oviscousin [Wisconsin River], where we hoped La Salle would send a reinforcement of Frenchmen with powder, lead and other munitions, as he had promised on our departure from the Illinois. The Sioux agreed to allow this voyage, provided that Michel Accault stay behind with them. So Picard and I went in a wretched, little canoe toward the Wisconsin. Our whole stock consisted of 15 charges of powder, a gun, an earthen pot, a knife and a beaver robe, with which to travel 500 miles.

We portaged our canoe at the Falls of St. Anthony, [at the site of Minneapolis]. This cataract is wonderful and frightful, falling 30 or 40 feet. At the falls we saw one of the Sioux, who had climbed an oak tree. He offered a well-dressed beaver robe as a sacrifice to the falls, saying to it, "You who are a spirit, grant that the men of our nation may pass here quietly, without accident; that we may kill many buffalo; that we may conquer our enemies and bring back slaves, some of whom we will put to death before you."

Two miles below the falls we saw a snake, six feet long, crawling up a cliff toward a swallow's nest to eat the young ones. We pelted him down with stones.

As we descended the Mississippi River we met some of our Sioux on an island, loaded with buffalo meat. Two hours after our landing, 15 or 16 Sioux warriors, whom we had left above the falls, entered with tomahawks in hand. They overthrew the lodge and took all the meat and bear oil. At first we took them to be enemies, but one, who called himself my uncle, said the others had broken the code of their nation, by putting the buffalo to flight before the mass of the nation had arrived.

As Picard and I canoed 150 miles down the Mississippi, we killed only one deer which was swimming across, and the heat was so great that the meat spoiled in one day. This made us look for turtles, which we found hard to take. We did take one, much larger than the rest, with a thinner shell and fatter meat. As I was trying to cut off his head, he all but bit off one of my fingers. Yet never have I

89

more admired God's providence. Eagles, which are very common in this vast country, sometimes dropped fish from their claws, which we recovered and ate.

We finally reached the mouth of the Wisconsin River, but finding no Frenchmen there, we turned back upstream to again ascend the Mississippi. We had only ten charges of powder left, which we divided into 20 to kill wild pigeons. When these gave out, we caught two catfish with hook and line.

We met our band of Sioux coming down from Buffalo River [Chippewa River] with their flotilla of canoes loaded with meat. We again went down the Mississippi to hunt with this multitude of canoes. From time to time the Indians hid their canoes on the river bank, and struck out onto the prairies 18 or 20 miles beyond the bluffs. They killed, at different times, as many as 120 buffalo. They always left some of their old men on the bluff tops, to watch for their enemies.

One day the old men on duty cried out that they saw two warriors in the distance. The Sioux bowmen hurried there, each trying to outstrip the others, but they brought back only two women of their own nation. These women came to report that a party of Sioux, hunting near the western end of Lake Superior, had discovered five spirits—for so they call the French. The Frenchmen were told about us. They expressed a wish to come on, to learn whether we were English, Dutch, Spanish or French. They could not understand how we had reached the Sioux by so wide a journey.

On July 25th, 1680, as we were ascending the Mississippi River after the buffalo hunt, we met the Sieur de Luth [Daniel Greysolon Duluth] with four French soldiers. Duluth begged us to go with him to the villages of the Sioux, because we understood a little of their language. This I readily did, knowing that he and his soldiers had not approached the sacraments for two years.

Toward the end of September we told the Sioux that we had to return to our French settlements. The great chief consented and traced on paper the route we were to take for 1,000 miles.

We descended Rum River, then the Mississippi, then ascended Wisconsin River, which is as wide as the Illinois, with a strong current.

90

After 150 miles on the Wisconsin, we came to a portage of a mile [at the site of Portage, Wisconsin]. The next day we crossed over to a river which winds wonderfully [Fox River]. We passed four lakes, where we found Mascoutens, Kickapoos and Foxes, growing Indian corn. All this country is as fine as that of the Illinois.

At last, 1,000 miles from the country of the Sioux, we arrived safely at Green Bay, where we found Frenchmen trading with the Indians.

TOILSOME JOURNEY

Anonymous   1680

In February of 1680, as Father Hennepin embarked for the Sioux Country, La Salle himself was preparing for an even more grueling journey. La Salle planned to travel on foot across the wilderness, all the way from Lake Peoria in the Illinois Country to Fort Frontenac on the northeast coast of Lake Ontario. The following episode is from an account by an anonymous author, submitted to the King of France in 1682.

During Father Hennepin's voyage, Monsieur de la Salle encountered new troubles. He had finished Fort Crevecœur [near Lake Peoria] and prepared timber for building a ship, but still he needed iron, ropes and sails. Meanwhile he reflected that summer was coming on, and that if he spent more months in useless waiting, his enterprise would be delayed a year, perhaps more. If he waited he would be unable to put his financial affairs in order, or to obtain the articles he needed.

In this crisis he formed a plan as extraordinary as it was difficult to carry out, namely, to go on foot all the way to Fort Frontenac, a distance of more than 1,300 miles.

The winter had been severe. The ground was covered with snow, neither melted nor firm enough to bear up a man on snowshoes. La Salle would need to carry the usual outfit: a blanket, linen, a kettle, a hatchet, a gun, powder and ball, and dressed skins to make moccasins, which last but a day. (French shoes are of no service in this country.) La Salle had to make up his mind to push through thickets and brushwood; to wade for whole days, sometimes waist-deep in marsh-water and melted snow; to go sometimes without eating, because he could carry no food; to run the risk, day and night, of being surprised by some band of the four or five nations who were at war along his route. But all these difficulties did not deter him. His only care was to find among his people some men resolute enough to go with him.

On the 17th of February, two chiefs of the Matoutenta tribe, who live 200 or 250 miles west of the Great River [Mississippi River], came to see the Frenchmen. One of these had at his belt a horse's hoof and skin of part of the leg, serving as a pouch. He said he had brought it from a country five or six days' journey west of his own, where the inhabitants had long hair and fought on horseback with lances. These details indicated that he spoke of the Spaniards in New Mexico. This new information increased La Salle's desire to complete his discoveries, and persuaded him to carry out his plan.

Leaving Monsieur de Tonty in command of the fort, La Salle set out on the 1st of March with six of his strongest men and one savage in two canoes. Near the fort the current kept the [Illinois] river clear of ice, but after traveling three miles and reaching a lake [Lake Peoria], they found it frozen over. Unwilling to abandon his canoes, La Salle told his men to make two sleds, upon which they placed their loaded canoes and dragged them over the snow to the end of the lake. The next morning they found the river covered with ice too weak to walk upon, but too strong for bark canoes to break through. They were forced to carry their canoes and equipage ten miles through the woods, constantly mid-leg deep in snow. At nightfall they reached huts of savages, where they were sheltered from a heavy rain that fell all night.

On the 3rd of March they again embarked upon the river, which they found covered with ice in places where they had to break a passage with poles. In the afternoon they found ice more than a foot thick, but having such inequalities and holes that they could not walk upon it, so they were forced to make a circuit of almost five miles, and to drag their canoes over frozen swamps. Beyond the swamps the river was open, and they paddled until they were forced to land to let masses of ice float by. This they repeated several times until nightfall. The following day they continued their journey, sometimes paddling, sometimes breaking ice with flails and hatchets, sometimes dragging the canoes through the water, sometimes dragging them over snow through the woods. The next evening they were stopped by a heavy snowfall. On the 9th of March, the snow being frozen, they set out on snowshoes. That day and the next they made 45 or 50 miles, and they finally reached the great village of the Illinois [near the site of Utica, Illinois].

During the next two days a heavy rain loosened the ice in the river, but this ice was stopped by the islands and bars. It formed great jams and piled up with prodigious noise, so that La Salle lost hope of being able to send food back to the fort immediately. Indeed, he found no one at the village of the Illinois from whom to buy food. Seeing tracks in the snow, he thought there must be some Illinois hunting in the neighborhood. He set fire to frost-dried reeds, hoping that the smoke, which could be seen at a great distance in that open country, would attract a savage. He was not disappointed. The next day La Salle, having left camp while his men were smoke-drying the flesh of a buffalo, saw two savages approaching, closely followed by Chassagoac, the principal and most friendly chief of the Illinois. Giving him a red blanket, a kettle, hatchets and knives, La Salle told him that the Frenchmen at the fort needed food, and begged him to furnish them some. Chassagoac promised to use all his influence in favor of the French, and to load Indian corn into a canoe which La Salle would leave with two of his men, who would take the corn back to the fort. They then had a long conversation. La Salle promised to return soon with a large supply of arms and goods. La Salle said that after he discovered the mouth of the Mississippi River, he would send more Frenchmen to establish a colony among the Illinois.

Meanwhile the four Frenchmen and the savage carried La Salle's canoe and his goods to a rapids ten miles above the village. There he joined them, and as the river was open, they embarked and traveled 32 miles on the 16th and 17th, although masses of floating ice frequently forced them to land. On the 18th they found the river so solidly frozen that La Salle gave up hope of further progress by canoe. He and his men hid the canoe on an island and set out on foot, burdened with their whole outfit. In two days they crossed a prairie 70 miles wide, marching constantly through water from snow melted by the strong, midday sun.

All of the 21st and until noon of the 22nd they continued their journey through great swamps, beyond which flowed a deep, swift stream. Wishing to make a raft, they found no wood except oak, which was unsuited for their purpose. Choosing the drier branches and filling in with bundles of reeds, they fastened the whole by means of withes, and so passed over the stream in water up to their knees. On the 23rd they crossed three other streams in the same manner. That evening they reached the shore of the Lake of the Illinois [Lake Michigan] and on the 24th they reached the Miami River [St. Joseph River], where La Salle found the fort he had built the preceding fall, [near the site of Benton Harbor, Michigan]. He then continued his eastward course toward Lake Erie, through forests so thickly interlaced with thorns and brambles that in two and a half days he and his men had their clothing torn to shreds, and their faces so scratched and bloody that they were not recognizable.

On the 28th they came to fine woods where they found plenty of food. Before that time they had lacked food more than once, and had often been forced to march until nightfall without eating. From this point on they suffered no lack, either of small game or of venison. No sooner had they killed a deer, a bear or a turkey, than they roasted a portion, eating it without bread, wine or salt. They were in a country where the savages did not go to hunt, as it was the borderland between five or six nations who were at war and who did not enter it save by stealth, in order to surprise and kill some of their enemies. As a result, the shots fired by the Frenchmen and the carcasses they left behind soon put some of the barbarians upon their trail.

95

On the evening of the 28th a band of Wapoos followed them and discovered them, because of a fire which they had started on the edge of a beautiful prairie. Those barbarians had already surrounded them, and would certainly have taken them by surprise had not the Frenchman on guard awakened the rest, whereupon each man quickly slipped behind a tree, gun in hand. The savages mistook them for Iroquois, and thinking them to be in great force because they did not conceal their march, the savages took flight without firing their arrows, fearing to be surrounded themselves. They spread such an alarm on all sides that the Frenchmen met no one for two days.

Perceiving their terror and guessing the reason for their flight, La Salle left marks like those an army of Iroquois would have made, lighting several campfires and drawing slaves and scalps on the bark of trees, according to the custom of the Iroquois. Being in the middle of this prairie and thinking to conceal his trail, La Salle set fire to the dry grass which grew on all sides. He made use of this strategy until they reached the end of the open country. On the 30th they came to great swamps flooded by the thaw, and were obliged to cross in mud and water to the waist. The tracks they left soon made their number known to a band of Mascoutens who were on the lookout for Iroquois. During the three days they waded through the swamps, the Mascoutens followed them, but could not overtake them, because the Frenchmen made no fires—simply taking off their wet clothes upon some high knoll to dry overnight while they slept in their blankets. But on the night of April 2nd, the frost was so heavy that they were forced to light a fire in order to dry their frozen clothes. The fire revealed them to the Mascoutens, who were not far off, and who came running with loud yells to within a hundred paces of the Frenchmen. La Salle advanced to within gunshot of them, whereupon, either restrained by the sight of firearms, or perhaps recognizing their error, the savages called out that they were brothers of the Frenchmen. The savages said they had mistaken the French for Iroquois.

La Salle continued his journey until the 4th of April, when two of his exhausted men fell sick and were unable to walk. It became necessary to look for a river flowing toward Lake Erie, and to build a canoe. Finding a suitable stream, they felled an elm tree from which the bark could be peeled by the constant application of boiling water. Making a canoe from the elm, they soon embarked. Navigation was interrupted by trees that had fallen across the bed of the stream, frequently forcing them to land. The course of the stream was so winding that in five days they found they had not gone as far as they could go on foot in a single day. As the sick men began to feel better, they abandoned the canoe, and in a few days safely reached the bank of the Detroit River, through which Lake Huron pours into Lake Erie.

Here La Salle left two of his men, directing them to make a canoe and go to Missilimakinak [Mackinac]. Then, accompanied by two Frenchmen and the savage, he crossed the Detroit River on a raft. They followed the shore of Lake Erie on foot, but the thaw and continual rains flooded almost all the woods through which they marched. One of La Salle's men and the savage were seized with a severe fever and inflammation of the lungs, so that they spat blood. This forced La Salle, with the help of the one man who remained healthy, to build a canoe to carry the sick. Finishing it within two days and embarking on Lake Erie, they reached Niagara on the 21st of April, the day after Easter. Here La Salle found some Frenchmen who had wintered in a cabin above the falls.

La Salle's men being no longer able to follow him, he took with him three fresh men from the falls and pushed on. Continual rains caused him much delay, so that he was unable to reach Fort Frontenac until the 6th of May, thus finishing a journey of more than 1,300 miles—the most toilsome that any Frenchman has ever undertaken in America.

WE ARE ALL SAVAGES

Anonymous   1680

La Salle was in Montreal in July of 1680, preparing to return to his wilderness fort, when bad news reached him from the far-distant Illinois Country.

Messengers brought word of the desertion of the shipwrights, the blacksmith, the joiner and most of the others. In the absence of Monsieur de Tonty, they had pillaged the storehouse, carrying off peltries, goods and munitions. They had overthrown the palisade of the fort, leaving their commander helpless and defenseless.

La Salle made haste to depart, in order to help Monsieur de Tonty. On the 10th of August, 1680, La Salle set out from Fort Frontenac upon his second journey to the Illinois Country. He had with him shipwrights to finish the vessel he had begun at Fort Crevecœur. He followed the north shore of Lake Huron to Missi-limakinak [Mackinac] where he was surprised to hear no word of Tonty. La Salle was anxious, for he knew that Tonty was destitute of everything. He also knew that the Iroquois had gone on the warpath against the Illinois.

At Mackinac, La Salle awaited the arrival of a blacksmith, a rope maker and two soldiers who were to bring 300 pounds of powder, lead, guns, iron, oakum, resin, sails and tools for finishing his vessel. However, violent winds that autumn prevented them from reaching

Mackinac. Finally, on October 4th, La Salle set out with 12 men. He was so impeded by wind and rain that he did not reach the mouth of the Miami River [St. Joseph River on the south coast of Lake Michigan] until November 4th. There La Salle left his heavy cargo in charge of the carpenter and five others, and set off with six Frenchmen and one savage. On November 16th he reached the portage between the St. Joseph River and the Teatiki [Kankakee River, near the site of South Bend, Indiana]. Pushing on, he found the game very abundant. This gave much pleasure to his men, but it worried La Salle, because he could not imagine what had prevented the Illinois from setting fire to the prairies, as usual, to hunt buffalo.

On the 27th La Salle arrived at the junction of the Divine River [Des Plaines River] and the Kankakee, where he landed to look for signs of the passage of Tonty, who could have returned only by ascending one of these two rivers. Finding no sign, La Salle was convinced that Tonty would be at the great village of the Illinois. Delighted with this hope, La Salle stopped at the junction of the rivers for three days to hunt. His men killed 12 very fat buffalo, eight deer and many turkeys, geese and swans. Being but 40 miles from the village, where he supposed all to be well, La Salle had all the meats dried, intending to preserve them for the winter's supply. He then loaded a canoe with the choicest parts, thinking to celebrate his arrival with a feast to Tonty and the other loyal Frenchmen.

On December 1st La Salle finally arrived at the great village of the Illinois [near the site of Utica, Illinois]. There he was astounded to find no lodges at all, but only charred stakes. Upon most of the stakes he saw the heads of dead savages, placed there to be devoured by crows. La Salle recognized in this the signs of rage of an invading Iroquois army. He found more skulls at the gates of an Iroquois fort, along with a mass of burnt bones and some remains of French utensils and clothing. In the fields he saw many human carcasses, half gnawed by wolves. He saw Illinois tombs destroyed, and the bones dragged from the graves and scattered about the prairie. The trenches in which the Illinois hid their implements were all opened, and kettles and pots were broken. He saw half-burnt heaps of Indian corn. The

99

horror of the scene was increased by the howls of wolves and the screams of crows.

It is easy to imagine La Salle's astonishment at this spectacle. He walked around the Iroquois fort, where he found no marks of gunshots or arrows, nor any sign that the French had been imprisoned there. One after another he inspected all the heads of the dead. It was not a pleasant business, but he was bound to do it, to learn the fate of Tonty and his men. La Salle recognized all the heads to be those of Illinois savages, with coarse, close-cropped hair. Finally, coming by chance to the garden of the French, he found six stakes set up, painted red, and each bearing the black image of a man with his eyes bandaged. As it is the custom of the savages to set up stakes in the places where they have taken or slain their enemies, this led him to think that the Iroquois, finding six Frenchmen by themselves, had massacred or enslaved them. La Salle also saw many fresh footprints of savages. However, the severe cold compelled him to make a great fire and to remain there with his men, who took turns all night in keeping a sharp lookout.

La Salle passed a sleepless night, filled with grief, fearing the unhappy consequences of so many unexpected events, and not knowing what course to take. At length he decided to push on with four men, leaving the other three with the supplies, so that he might not be impeded in his course. Everything he left behind was hidden in a cavern, very hard of access, and the cavern was sealed in such a way that nothing could be harmed. Finally he gave orders for the three men who would remain to retire to a neighboring island. He told them to make no smoke during the day, nor to fire their guns, and to hide their canoes in the undergrowth. He pointed out that the savages would not swim over to attack an unknown number of men, and this island, being between two rapids, could be attacked only in the daytime, and only at the eastern point, where he urged his men to keep a sharp lookout.

On the next day, the 2nd of December, La Salle embarked in the afternoon, with Autray, You, Hunaut and a savage. Each man had two guns, a pistol, a sword, powder and ball, and knives and hatchets for gifts. Traveling 16 miles before nightfall, they reached the place where the Illinois had first sent their women and children to hide from the Iroquois. It was a landspit 15 or 20 paces wide and one mile in length; protected on one side by the river and on the other by a vast muddy morass. There remained an entrance only four paces wide, which was closed by great fallen trees. This whole peninsula was full of the huts of savages. Their dug-out canoes had made a kind of parapet along the river, the only side from which they could have been attacked. La Salle inspected the whole ground, but found no sign of conflict.

Directly across the river, La Salle saw the signs of an Iroquois encampment of 113 lodges. Upon the bark of trees he found portraits of their chiefs, and a statement of the number of warriors led by each. There were 582 warriors in all, one of whom was shown pierced by a gunshot, and nine wounded by arrows. Also pictured were an Illinois woman and the scalps of 11 others whom they had killed, but there was no sign of the French.

La Salle and his men set out very early the next morning and traveled that day about 80 miles [down the Illinois River]. On their way, they examined six camp sites of the Illinois and as many of the Iroquois. The Iroquois each night had camped just across the river from the Illinois. At none of these camp sites did La Salle see any sign of the French. Late that day, they arrived at Pimiteoui [Lake Peoria] and Fort Crevecœur.

At Crevecœur La Salle found that his fort had been almost entirely demolished by the French deserters, and that the Iroquois had pulled nails out of the vessel to show they had passed. He also found a broken piece of board inscribed with the words WE ARE ALL SAVAGES.

The next day La Salle set off again, passing on that day four more pairs of camp sites for the two armies. At the last, he judged that the two nations were not far distant, because no rain had fallen on the ashes of their camp fires. All that night La Salle and his four men pushed on.

The next day at about noon, as they neared the mouth of the river, La Salle saw figures resembling men and children, but motionless. Going ashore, he found all the grass trodden down, and a little to one side, the body of a woman half burnt and eaten by wolves. From this he could easily infer the rest, and judge the outcome of the war. This whole plain was covered with horrible traces of Iroquois cruelty. It would be impossible to describe the ferocity of those madmen, and the tortures they had inflicted upon the miserable Illinois. Parts of bodies had been left in kettles over fires. The Iroquois had put those hapless people to death by a thousand tortures. What he had seen from a distance proved to be heads and entire bodies, impaled and roasted, and then set up in the field. There were also shields hanging upon stakes, to serve as trophies of the Iroquois. But after a careful and sorrowful search, La Salle found nothing to make him think that the Frenchmen had been involved in this disaster.

To neglect nothing that might offer a clue, La Salle went on as far as the Mississippi River, but found no trace of either the French or the savages. Then, hewing branches from a little tree growing at the mouth of the Illinois River, he nailed to it a bit of board. On this he depicted his canoe and a peace pipe, and fastened to it a letter informing Tonty of his return, telling Tonty that he would find hidden near the Illinois village some hatchets, knives and other articles necessary in case he was among the savages. La Salle hoped that a passing savage would bear this letter to Tonty.

La Salle's men now proposed to descend the Mississippi River to the sea, offering to risk their lives for the sake of satisfying his passionate wish to carry out this discovery. He praised their courage, but told them he would not take advantage of it. They were too few, he explained, to try to go among so many nations. Their action would be judged to be the fruit of rashness or despair. They had not enough ammunition. He said they could carry out the plan with more safety the following year. Moreover, La Salle could not forsake the three men who had been left at the great Illinois village, nor could he abandon the search for Tonty without learning what had become of him.

ARM OF IRON

Henri de Tonty   1680

La Salle continued to hope that his trusted follower, Henri de Tonty, had survived the Iroquois onslaught. Tonty, who was Italian by birth, had just one hand— the other had been blown off by a grenade during a battle in Sicily. In its place Tonty brandished an iron hand. The Indians called him Bras de Fer, *or "Arm of Iron." La Salle wrote of Tonty, "Perhaps you would not think him capable of doing things for which both hands seem absolutely necessary. Yet his energy and skill make him equal to anything."*

While I was away from the fort, my men deserted, leaving me with just two Franciscan priests and three other Frenchmen, newly arrived from France. The mutineers stripped us of everything that was finest and most valuable, including ammunition. They left us at the mercy of the savages.

Meanwhile, the Illinois were greatly alarmed at the arrival of their most dreaded enemy, a war party of 600 Iroquois. The Illinois suspected that we had betrayed them to the Iroquois, because of the desertion of our men and the departure of La Salle. They angrily blamed me for the arrival of the Iroquois. This embarrassed me, as I myself had recently arrived from France and was not familiar with their manners.

103

I decided to go to the Iroquois enemy with a necklace of beads as a gift, and I took an Illinois warrior with me. As we separated from the other Illinois warriors, 400 in number, they were already fighting the enemy. As we approached within gun-shot of the Iroquois, they fired a great volley at us, compelling me to tell the Illinois warrior to go back. He did so.

As I reached the Iroquois, those wretches seized me, snatched the necklace from my hand, and one of them plunged a knife into my chest, wounding a rib near my heart. I began to bleed both from the wound and from my mouth. Recognizing me, the Iroquois then carried me into the middle of their camp and asked me why I had come to them. I made them understand that the Illinois were under the protection of the King of France and the Governor of New France; I was surprised that the Iroquois wished to break with the French and delay peace. I overstated the strength of the Illinois, saying they had 1,200 warriors, along with other savages and 60 French.

All this time the two sides were fighting. An Iroquois warrior came to tell his chief that their left wing was giving way. He also said he had recognized some Frenchmen fighting alongside the Illinois. At this the Iroquois were greatly angered at me and held a council to decide what to do with me. A man with a knife in his hand stood behind me, and from time to time lifted up my hair. They were divided in opinion. Tegancouti, chief of the Seneca Iroquois, wished positively to have me burned. Agonstat, chief of the Onondaga Iroquois and a friend of La Salle's, wished to have me set free. Agonstat carried his point. They agreed that, to better deceive the Illinois, they should send me back with a necklace of beads, to show that they too were children of the governor, and that the two nations should unite and make peace.

I had much trouble reaching the Illinois, because of my great loss of blood. On my way I met the fathers Gabriel de la Ribourde and Zenoble Membre, who were coming to look after me. They expressed their joy that the Iroquois had not put me to death. Together we went to the Illinois, where I repeated the message, but I added that they should not entirely trust the Iroquois. Seeing the Iroquois always in battle array, the Illinois decided to rejoin their

104

wives and children, eight miles away. They left us—two fathers, three Frenchmen and myself—at the mercy of the Iroquois.

The Iroquois then built a fort [near the site of Utica, Illinois] and left us in a cabin some distance from their fort. Two days later the Illinois again appeared on the hills within sight of the Iroquois who pressed me to convince the Illinois to come and make peace. The Iroquois gave me one of their warriors as a hostage, and I took him to the Illinois. He remained with them, and one of the Illinois warriors returned with me. When we reached the Iroquois fort, instead of mending matters, the Illinois warrior spoiled things entirely, by telling the enemy that his people had only 400 warriors, that the rest of their young men were all gone to war, and that they were ready to give beaver skins and slaves, if the Iroquois would make peace. At this, the Iroquois loaded me with accusations. They said I was a liar to have told them the Illinois had 1,200 warriors and several tribes of allies. They asked me where the 60 Frenchmen were. I had great trouble in getting out of the scrape.

That evening they sent the Illinois warrior back, to tell his nation to come the next day to make peace. The next day at noon the Iroquois gave three necklaces to the Illinois. The first necklace signified that the Governor of New France was not angry at their coming to molest their brothers. The second necklace was addressed to La Salle, with the same meaning. The third necklace bound them by oath to an alliance with the Illinois. The two nations then separated.

The Illinois believed in the peace, and several times they went into the fort of the enemy. But when some of the Illinois chiefs asked me what I thought, I said that they had everything to fear, that there was no good faith among the Iroquois barbarians, and that I knew the Iroquois were making canoes of elm bark in which they could pursue the Illinois. I told the Illinois that they should take advantage of the time and retire to some distant country, for they most certainly would be betrayed.

On the eighth day after their arrival, the Iroquois called Father Zenoble and myself to council. Setting six packets of beaver pelts before us, they said the first two packets were to tell the governor they would not eat his children [the Illinois] and that he should not be angry at what they had done. The third was to help heal my wound. The fourth was for rubbing oil on our limbs, to relieve us after our journey. The fifth was to signify that the sun is bright; the sixth, that we should leave the next day for the French settlements. I then asked them when they themselves would go away. Murmurs arose among them. A few answered that they would eat some of the Illinois before they went away. At that I kicked away their presents. I said there was no use making presents to me. I would have none of their presents, because they planned to eat the children of the governor. The Iroquois were angered, and the chiefs, rising, drove me from the council.

We went to our lodge where we passed the night on guard, resolved to kill some of them before they killed us. We thought we would not live through the night. However, at daybreak, they ordered us to depart, and we did so.

> *Tonty's suspicions of treachery proved to be well-founded. The Iroquois soon attacked the Illinois (as witnessed by La Salle, and described in the preceding chapter). As for the injured Tonty and his small band of Frenchmen, they faced the hardships of a long winter journey, in just a single small canoe, with little food or ammunition. The nearest French outpost was the Jesuit mission at Green Bay, 300 miles away.*

After paddling for 35 miles up the Illinois River, we landed to dry some pelts. While we were repairing our canoe, Father Gabriel said he was going aside to pray. I advised him not to go, because we were surrounded by enemies. He went off, and when he did not return, I went to look for him with one of my men. We found only his trail, cut by several others, which then joined into one. I brought back this sad news to Father Zenoble, who was greatly grieved at it.

Toward evening we made a great fire, hoping that perhaps Father Gabriel might return. As it burned, we crossed over to the other side of the river, where we kept a sharp lookout. Toward midnight we saw a man appear, then many others. The next day we recrossed the river. After waiting till noon, we embarked for the Lake of the Illinois [Lake Michigan], traveling by short journeys, always hoping to meet with the good father. We later learned that Father Gabriel, having walked 1,000 paces away from us, had been surrounded by 40 savages of the Kickapoo nation who had carried him away and broken his head.

We reached Lake Michigan and embarked northward. On November 1st we were wrecked, 55 miles from the Potawatomi village [north of the site of Milwaukee].

As our food failed us, we set off by land; but I ran a fever constantly and my legs were swollen, so we did not arrive at the village of the Potawatomies until November 14th. During that time we lived on nothing but wild garlic, which we had to grub up from under the snow.

When we arrived at the Potawatomi village [near the site of Kewaunee, Wisconsin] we were distressed to find no savages. They had left for their winter hunting grounds. We were obliged to go into their old garden beds, where we gleaned just a few handfuls of Indian corn and some frozen gourds, which we piled up in a hut at the lake shore. While we were gleaning in the wilds, one of our Frenchmen arrived with our canoe. He entered the hut where we had left our little store of food, and thinking we had put the food there for him, he ate much of it. When we returned we were very much surprised to find him in the hut. We had much pleasure in seeing him, but much regret in seeing most of our food eaten.

Now we could no longer delay, so we embarked in the canoe, but after six miles, the wind forced us ashore. There we saw a fresh trail, and I ordered that we follow it. It was the trail of the Potawatomies, who had made a portage to La Baye des Puants [Green Bay]. The next day, weak as we were, we carried our little canoe and all our things for three miles across the portage and into the bay. We embarked on a creek called Sturgeon Creek [Sturgeon Bay] and then risked turning to the right, not knowing where to go. Sixteen miles further we were stopped by the wind, and we were forced to eat the little food we still had.

107

At last we held a council to decide what we should do. Despairing of not being able to find the savages, everyone asked to return to the deserted Indian village. With wood there, we would at least be warm as we died.

The wind lulled and we set off, but on entering Sturgeon Bay we saw the creek had frozen in the night. Having no leather, we made shoes from the late Father Gabriel's cloak. We planned to start our march the next morning.

In the morning, as I was urging my weakened men to set off, two Ottawa savages appeared before us, and soon led us to the Potawatomies. I spent the winter with them, and Father Zenoble left us to spend the winter with the Jesuit fathers at the end of Green Bay.

In May of 1681, Tonty and La Salle were finally re-united at Mackinac. Despite their past failures and hardships, the two men began to lay plans for a new expedition to discover the mouth of the Mississippi River. A Frenchman wrote of their meeting, "Anyone else would have thrown up his hands and abandoned the enterprise, but far from this, I saw La Salle more determined than ever to continue his work and push forward his discovery."

The next year La Salle and Tonty at last succeeded in descending the Mississippi River to the Gulf of Mexico. There, in the name of King Louis of France, La Salle claimed possession of "this Country of Louisiana, drained by the River Mississippi and all the rivers that flow into it, from its source beyond the country of the Nadouessioux [Sioux] as far as its mouth at the Gulf of Mexico, upon the assurance we have from the natives of these countries that we are the first Europeans to have descended the River Mississippi."

PLENTITUDE

Joutel 1684–85

The Illinois wilderness held great promise for the French. They were attracted there by friendly natives, a milder climate, teeming game, fertile soil, and the beauty of the open prairies. In August of 1684, a veteran French soldier named Joutel approached the Illinois Country from the south, as he and his companions ascended the Mississippi River.

Our toil was great, for we were obliged to paddle the canoe to help our savages stem the current of the river, which was very strong and swift. We were often forced to land, sometimes to travel over miry lands where we sank halfway up the leg, other times over burning sands which scorched our feet, other times over splinters of wood which ran into the soles of our feet. We had to gather wood to dry our meat and to provide all things for our savages, who would not do so much as fetch a cup of water, even though we were on the bank of the river. Yet we were happy enough to have them with us.

On the 7th we saw a buffalo bull. The savages, who had a great mind to eat flesh, made a sign to me to go kill him. I pursued him and shot, but he did not fall. The savages then ran after the buffalo, but before they killed him, they performed a ceremony. First they adorned his head with swan's down and goose down, dyed red. Then they put tobacco in his nostrils and between the clefts of his hooves. After they killed him, they cut out the tongue and put a bit of tobacco in its place. Then they stuck two wooden forks in the ground and

109

laid a stick across them, from which they hung several slices of flesh, in the nature of an offering. This ceremony ended, we dried the best parts of the beast, and proceeded on our journey.

On the 19th we came to the mouth of a river called Houabache [Ohio River], said to come from the country of the Iroquois, toward New England. It is a very fine river, its water extraordinarily clear, its current gentle. Our savages offered to it a sacrifice of some tobacco and buffalo meat, which they fixed on forks and left on the bank, to be disposed of as the river thought fit.

We observed other superstitions among those poor people. On certain days, they fasted. We recognized those days when, as soon as they awoke, they smeared their faces and bodies with a shiny sort of earth or pounded charcoal. All that day they would not eat until late night. They fasted so that they might succeed in hunting, and kill many buffalo.

We held our course, and on the 25th, the savages showed us a spring of salt water. The ground around it was much beaten by buffalo hooves. The buffalo seem to love the salt water. The country was full of oaks and walnuts, plum trees and other sorts of fruit trees. On the 27th we saw another herd of buffalo and went ashore to kill some. We saved the best of the buffalo flesh. We held our course until evening, when we noticed a change in the humor and behavior of our savages. One of them told us they intended to leave us, which obliged us to secure our arms and double our watch during the night, for fear they would forsake us.

On the 1st of September we passed by the mouth of a river called Missouri. Its water is always thick. Our savages did not forget to offer a sacrifice to this river.

On the 2nd we arrived at a rock on which is painted the figure of the monster spoken of by Father Marquette [at the site of Alton, Illinois]. The monster consists of two scurvy figures drawn in red on the flat side of the rock. Our savages paid homage by offering a sacrifice to the rock, although we tried to make them understand that the rock had no virtue, and that we worshipped something above it, pointing to heaven. But it was to no purpose. They made signs to us that they would die if they did not perform their duty.

110

We proceeded, coasting along a chain of bluffs, and at length, on the 3rd, we left the Mississippi River to enter the River of the Illinois. We found a great change in that river, as its current is very gentle. The country is much more beautiful and agreeable, by reason of the many fine woods and fruits that adorn its banks. It was a great comfort to find such ease in going up that river, by reason of its gentle stream. We went on without stopping any longer than to kill a buffalo.

On the 10th we crossed a lake called Primitehouy [Lake Peoria], and returned to the channel of the river. On the 11th we saw savages before us, encamped on the bank of the river. We stopped and made ready our arms. One of the them came toward us by land, and when he was near, he stood gazing at us without speaking. We made him understand that we were French, and he made signs that we should advance toward his people. As we approached, they fired several shots to salute us, and we answered them with our firelocks. We asked them what nation they were. They said they were Illinois, of a canton called Cascasquia [Kaskaskia]. They invited us to eat of such as they had, and they gave us some gourds and melons, in exchange for which we gave them some dried meat.

On Sunday, the 14th of September, we came into the neighborhood of Fort Louis [Fort St. Louis, a French fort near the site of Utica, Illinois]. We were met by savages on the bank, who ran to the fort to carry the news. Immediately, we saw a Frenchman come out with a company of savages who fired a volley to salute us. We went ashore, leaving one man in the canoe to watch our baggage, for the Illinois are very sharp at carrying off anything they can lay their hands on. We entered the fort and surprised several Frenchmen who had not expected us. We were then conducted to the chapel, where we gave thanks to God from the bottoms of our hearts, for having conducted us safely. All this while the savages came by intervals to fire their pieces, to express their joy for our arrival.

Our plan was to make the best of our way to Canada, there to set out aboard the first ship that sailed for France. Sieur Boisrondet (who had served as clerk to La Salle) told us he had a canoe in which he planned to go down to Canada, and we prepared to use that

Guarding the corn, by Seth Eastman

opportunity. We took care to gather furs for barter as we passed by Micilimaquinay [Mackinac].

It would be needless to relate all the troubles and hardships we met with on that journey. It was painful and fruitless, for after reaching the shore of the lake [Lake Michigan at the Chicago portage], we waited five days for the very foul weather to cease. We finally embarked on the lake, in spite of the storm, but we were forced to put ashore again and to return to Fort St. Louis, where we arrived the 7th of October. Thus we were obliged to stay at the fort all the rest of that autumn and part of the winter as well.

It was then the good season for hunting. The gentlemen at the fort had secured two savage huntsmen, who never let us want for wildfowl of all sorts. We had good bread made of Indian corn, and good fruit. If there had been anything to drink besides water, we would have fared well. The leisure we had during our stay allowed me to observe the Illinois Country.

Fort St. Louis sits on a steep rock [Starved Rock near Utica, Illinois], about 200 feet high, with the river running at its bottom. It is fortified with only a palisade of stakes, but it has a spacious esplanade or place for arms. The position is naturally strong, and could be further strengthened with little expense.

The country of the Illinois enjoys all advantages—not only beauty, but also a plentitude of all things needed to support human life. The prairie, which is watered by the river, is beautified by small hills covered with groves of oaks and walnut trees. The prairies are full of grass, growing very tall. The country is one of the most temperate in the world, so that whatever is grown there—whether herbs, roots, Indian corn or even wheat—grows very well. Sieur Boisrondet has sown wheat there and has had a plentiful crop.

As for the customs of the Illinois, they are naturally fierce and revengeful. Among them, the toil of sowing, planting, carrying burdens and all other tasks that support life are done by the women. The men have no other business than going to war or hunting. The women must fetch the game after the men have killed it, sometimes carrying it very far to their lodges, to dry it or dress it. When the corn is sown, the women protect it from the birds until it comes

113

up. These birds are a sort of starling, like ours in France, but they fly in great swarms.

The Illinois are extremely fond of their children. They never chide or beat them, but only throw water at them as punishment.

Unlike other nations, the Illinois are addicted to thieving. You must watch their feet as well as their hands, for they know how to turn anything away most nimbly. They are like all other savages in that they boast much of their warlike exploits. This is their main topic, and they are great liars.

They pay respect to their dead by their special care in burying them, even by putting the bodies of chiefs and other important persons in lofty coffins. While other nations weep for the dead and complain for days, the Illinois do just the contrary. When any of them dies, they wrap the body in skins, place it in a bark coffin, then sing and dance around it for a whole day. The dancers tie gourds to their bodies, which rattle and make noise. Some of them beat on a drum made of a great earthen pot with a deer skin stretched across it. During the rejoicing they throw gifts on the coffin, such as bracelets, pendants and strings of beads. When the ceremony is over, they bury the body with some of the gifts. They also bury a store of Indian corn with a pot to boil it in, so the dead person will not be hungry on his long journey.

On the 27th of October, Monsieur Tonty returned from war with the Iroquois. We embraced him and described our adventures.

We stayed there until the end of February when we decided to depart, although we had received no news from Canada. We set out from Fort St. Louis on the 21st of March, canoeing up the river, which was navigable by then. Before we advanced 15 miles, we came to a rapids which forced us to pull our canoes through the water. I hurt my foot against a rock in the water there, which troubled me for a long time. We had to go into the water often, and I suffered extremely.

We arrived at Chicago on the 29th, but bad weather forced us to stay there until April. There was little game in that place, and we had nothing to eat but our Indian corn. Yet we discovered a kind of manna, which was a great help to us. It was a sort of maple tree

114

in which we made cuts, from which flowed a sweet liquor. In this liquor we boiled our Indian corn, which made it delicious and sweet. In the woods we also found a sort of garlic, small onions, and some charvel that tasted like ours, but had a different leaf.

As the weather mended, we embarked again [on Lake Michigan] on the 5th of April. We kept to the west side to shun the Iroquois. We saw storms and swelling waves like those on the sea, but we arrived safely on the 15th at a river called Quinetonan [probably Milwaukee River]. There is a village nearby where the savages live all summer, but leave during the winter to go hunting.

The game is not there, as in other countries. We found nothing but very lean deer, and those rarely, because there are many wolves that play great havoc, taking and devouring great numbers of deer. When the wolves discover a herd of deer, they rouse them and set them running. The deer never fail to take to the first lake they come to. The wolves then guard the banks carefully, moving along the edges. The poor deer are soon pierced by the cold of the lake. They grow weary and get out quite benumbed, so they are easily taken by the wolves. We frequently saw wolves watching from the side of a lake. Sometimes, as the deer quit their sanctuary, we took them ourselves.

On the 28th we arrived at a Potawatomi village [at Green Bay] where we bought Indian corn. In that place there are some Frenchmen and four Jesuit fathers, who have a cabin well built with timber and enclosed with stakes. There are also some Hurons and Outahouacs [Ottawas] whom the fathers take care to instruct, but with much trouble, for those people are great libertines. Often there are none but a few women in the church. There we stayed all May and part of June. No man dared to venture further at that time, because of the war with the Iroquois.

On the 29th of July we at last arrived in Quebec. Father Anastasius took us to the monastery of his order, where we were most kindly received by the father-guardian. He expressed much joy to see us, and we still more for being in a place of safety, after so many perils and toils.

115

MISSION
TO THE ILLINOIS

Father Sebastian Rasles   1692–94

Jesuit priests were attracted to the Illinois Country by reports that the Illinois Indians were more receptive to Christianity than were other tribes. In 1692 Father Sebastian Rasles journeyed to the Illinois to continue a mission that had been started 20 years earlier by Father Marquette.

After three months in Quebec studying the Algonquin language, I embarked in a canoe to go to the Illinois Country, 1,200 miles distant. So long a voyage in those barbarous regions holds great risks and hardships. We had to cross vast lakes where storms are as frequent as on the ocean. We landed every night, but were lucky to find a flat rock on which to sleep. When it rained we crawled under the canoe. But the greatest dangers were on the rivers, particularly at rapids. There the canoe flies like an arrow, and if it hits a rock, it is dashed into a thousand pieces. This happened to some of my companions, but I escaped such a fate with the protection of Divine Goodness.

We faced hunger, for this kind of voyage allowed us to carry only a sack of Indian corn. When hunting failed, we had to search for a kind of leaf called *tripe de roche* [lichen], prepared by boiling or roasting. I suffered less from hunger than some of my companions, who were scattered by storms. I arrived first at Michilimackinak

[Mackinac] and I sent food to them which prevented their starving to death. They had gone seven days with no food except a crow, which they killed more by accident than by skill, for they could not hold themselves up.

The season was too far advanced to go on to the Illinois, so I wintered at Mackinac. Two of our missionaries were there, one among the Hurons and one among the Ottawas.

As soon as spring came I embarked for the Illinois, and after 40 days I entered the River of the Illinois [probably via the portage at Chicago]. Following this river for 130 miles, I arrived at the first village of the Illinois, which contained 300 lodges and four or five fires.

The Illinois cover themselves about the waist, and leave the rest of the body naked. They tattoo all kinds of figures on their bodies in place of clothes. Only for visits to our church do they clothe themselves, during the summer in a dressed skin, and during the winter in a skin with fur on it. They put colored feathers on their heads, arranging garlands and crowns with great taste. They paint their faces with colors, mostly red. From their ears they hang small stones, some red, others blue, others white as alabaster.

When the Illinois are not at war or the hunt, they pass their time in sports, feasting or dancing. They have two kinds of dances: one to rejoice, attended by women and girls, the other to grieve the death of some important person. All may mourn a death, provided they give presents. They do not bury the dead, but rather wrap them in hides and attach them by the head and feet to the tops of trees.

When not involved in games, feasts or dances, the men remain on their mats, sleeping or making bows, arrows and pipes. As for the women, they work like slaves. In summer they cultivate the earth and plant Indian corn. In winter they make mats, dress skins and provide everything necessary for their lodge.

Of all the nations in Canada, none live in such abundance as the Illinois. Their rivers are covered with swans, geese, ducks and teal. With every mile one sees a multitude of turkeys in flocks as large as 200. These turkeys are much larger than those in France. I weighed one at 36 pounds. Bear and deer are found in great numbers. Buffalo

117

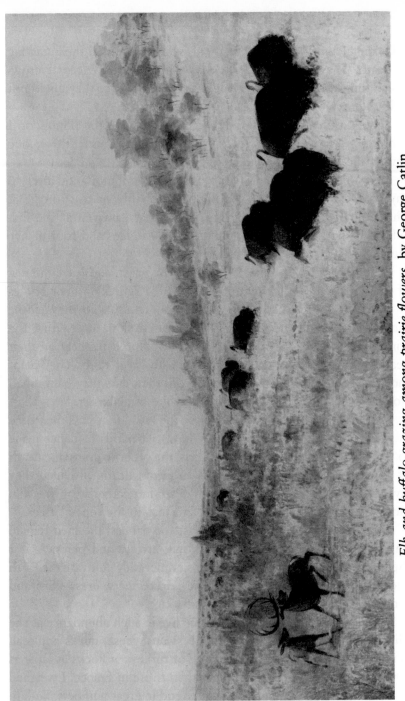

Elk and buffalo grazing among prairie flowers, by George Catlin

and elk are seen in vast herds. Each year the Illinois kill more than 2,000 buffalo. Four to five thousand buffalo can often be seen at once, grazing on the prairies. They have a hump on the back and a very large head. Their hair is curled and soft as wool. The meat is light, with a naturally salty taste. Even if eaten raw it does not cause indigestion. When the savages kill a buffalo that appears too lean, they take only the tongue and go in search of one that is fatter.

Arrows are the weapons the Illinois use most often in war and the hunt. These are pointed with stones sharpened in the shape of a snake's tongue. If no knife is at hand, they use arrow points to skin animals they have killed. They hardly ever miss their aim, and they can shoot a hundred arrows in the time it takes another to load his gun. They don't take the trouble to make fish nets, because of the abundance of animals. When they fancy to have fish, they stand upright in a canoe and shoot fish with an arrow.

The only way for an Illinois man to gain esteem is to be an able hunter or a good warrior. They passionately seek this kind of glory, and they don't hesitate to travel 1,000 miles through the depths of the forests to capture a slave or take the scalp of an enemy. They accept the fatigues and long fasts they must endure, particularly as they approach enemy territory. Then they do not dare to hunt, for fear a wounded animal with an arrow in its body might warn the enemy. They make war by surprising their enemy, so they send scouts ahead to learn the enemy's numbers, direction of travel and state of defense. They then set an ambush, or erupt into the enemy's lodge, tomahawk in hand, and kill some of them before they can defend themselves.

Their tomahawk is made of deer horn or wood in the shape of a short sword with a large ball at the end. They hold the tomahawk in one hand and a knife in the other. As soon as they deal a blow to the enemy's head, they cut it round with the knife and take the scalp with extraordinary speed.

When a warrior returns to his country with many scalps, he is greatly honored; but when he brings back prisoners, he is covered with glory. As soon as prisoners arrive, the people of the village line their path. The reception is most cruel. Some tear out nails, others

119

cut off fingers or ears, others deal blows with their clubs. After this reception the old men gather to decide whether the prisoners should live or die. When an Illinois warrior has been killed, they may decide the dead man should be replaced in his lodge, and so they give a prisoner to that lodge, to take the place of the dead warrior. They call this reviving the dead. When a prisoner is condemned to death, they plant a large post in the earth and tie the prisoner to it by both hands. They make him sing his death song, and all the savages sit about the stake. Each tortures according to his whim, all this taking four or five hours, and sometimes two or three days. The more shrill and piercing the cries, the more agreeable to those barbarians. It was the Iroquois who invented this frightful kind of death, and the Illinois treat their prisoners with the same cruelty, but only as retaliation.

It is a blessing for the Illinois that they are so distant from Quebec, because it is impossible to carry "fire water" [brandy] to them. This drink among the Indians is the greatest obstacle to Christianity. They never buy it without plunging into the most furious intoxication. The riots and sad deaths which we have witnessed should outweigh any gain made by the trade in a liquor so fatal.

120

MOST BEAUTIFUL COUNTRY

Father Antoine Silvy   1710–12

Like other Frenchmen before him, Father Antoine Silvy was impressed by the beauty and abundance of the Illinois Country. In 1710 he joined the Jesuit mission to the Illinois.

The Illinois Country is without doubt the most beautiful I have ever seen. The land is nearly flat, with some hillocks. As far as the eye can see there is prairie, broken only by scattered groves of trees: chestnut, acacia, oak, ash, white pine, beech, cottonwood, maple, walnut, mulberry, horse chestnut, elm and plum. All these trees are covered with vines bearing grapes.

Many animals live here: elk, deer, bear, lynx, beaver, otter, muskrat, buffalo and cougar. The cougar has a head like a cat, a long flanked belly, and a long tail. There are few animals it cannot catch. If cougars were as common as wolves, there would be few deer. There are also many kinds of game: hares, prairie chickens, wild pigeons, quail and turkeys. The marshes are full of waterfowl: geese, ducks, teal, swans and many others—so many that when drought forces them from the marshes, they cover the lakes and rivers. The Indians cannot pass in their canoes without clearing the way with their paddles.

In winter, the Illinois leave their villages to hunt for buffalo, elk, deer, beaver and bear. They live on the prairies rather than in the

121

woods, so they can see their enemies from a distance. When they find a herd of buffalo, the young men chase after them at a slow trot until they are within a half mile. Then they run with all their might to overtake them, shooting their muskets as well as countless arrows from their bows. Some buffalo fall, but the young hunters continue the chase and ambush the older buffalo, making a good killing. The men then take only the tongues and flat ribs. It is the women who must gather the rest of the meat, then smoke it and preserve it.

Toward the end of April they return to their village to plant crops: corn, beans, pumpkins and melons. They remain there all summer, making only short hunting trips from time to time.

To go hunting, they use large, dug-out, wooden canoes. No canoe of hunters would dare leave the main party, for others would go after it and destroy the canoe and its contents. Nor does any Indian wander from the group to hunt alone, for the others would pursue him and injure him. The reason is that a single hunter going ahead would put the animals to flight and force the group to travel farther to find food.

The Illinois make war in small groups of about 15 or 20 men. To form a war party, the war chief gives a feast, usually in February. He says the time is drawing near to go in search of men. It is time for them to pay homage to their birds. Each Indian has some kind of bird in which he places great confidence. Each keeps his own special birdskin in a case made of reeds. When the feast is done, the Indians sing to their birds during the night, to the sound of a rattle. One appeals to the crow, begging it to give him the same speed in pursuing his enemies. Another asks the falcon for the same strength against his enemies as the falcon has to kill other birds. When day breaks, they bring their birds to a council with the war chief. During a second feast, the chief tells them, "You know for a long time I have mourned my brother. He was killed by our enemies. Because we are comrades, he was your relative as well as mine. I alone am not strong enough to avenge my brother. I wait for your arms to give me the vengeance I demand. The birds assure me of our success. Their protection and your courage should make us risk everything."

After this speech, he rises and puts his hand on the head and shoulder of each of them. They say they are ready to set out, and they leave the following night.

As they travel, the war chief carries a mat containing the birds of all who march, as well as herbs and roots for dressing the wounded. They hide Indian corn in different spots along the way, so they will not be overloaded. This food will be eaten on the way back, so they will not have to rely on hunting.

When they reach the place where they expect to find their enemies, the leader takes all the birds from the mat and says a short prayer. He then sends out spies, and soon they attack the enemy, imitating the cries of their birds as they pursue them. They try to take prisoners, as this brings greater glory than taking scalps.

After the attack, the war chief makes a short speech, telling them to thank their spirits, then to leave with all speed. They march steadily for two or three days, both day and night. If one of their war party has been killed, the leader paints himself with earth and weeps as he marches. Arriving at the village he goes to see the family of the one killed, carrying a bow with broken arrows. He gives them gifts to cover the dead, and promises to avenge the death by attacking the enemy.

In the Illinois Country these war chiefs are not liked, as they are in other countries. Here they are hated by the family that has lost a relative. The Illinois have a saying: "A war chief cannot mend hearts with gifts."

123

CADILLAC'S MIRACLE

Antoine la Mothe de Cadillac   1702

*French settlements in the Upper Country were small
outposts in the wilderness: a trader's cabin, a crude
Jesuit chapel, a small fort enclosed by a palisade of
stakes. But in 1701, Antoine la Mothe de Cadillac arrived at Detroit River with the dream of founding a
new settlement that would some day rival Montreal as
a flourishing city. It was to be peopled by French settlers
and by thousands of Indians from all the nations of
the Upper Country. After his first year at Detroit, Cadillac wrote to the governor of New France to describe
in glowing terms the "miracle" of his new frontier settlement.*

Detroit is a river connecting Lake Huron and
Lake Erie, navigable throughout, so that a ship
of 100 guns could pass through safely. All
around this river are grand prairies with grass so high that a man can
scarcely be seen in it. Across the prairies are scattered large clusters
of trees, yet these trees are marvelously tall, and except for the great
oaks, have almost no branches but near the top. There are hazelnuts,
filberts and walnuts, trees good for furniture and gun stocks. There
are stretches of chestnut, mainly toward Lake Erie. In some places
the woods are mixed, with white and red oak, walnut, elm, bass-

124

wood, mulberry, cottonwood, chestnut and ash. Along the river banks and near the groves of timber are countless fruit trees, mostly plum and apple, that seem to form orchards as though planted by a gardener. On all sides are grape vines, some with bitter fruit, others with large and plump berries.

At the entrance to Lake Erie are boundless prairies which stretch away for 300 miles. There the mighty buffalo find pastures in abundance. Deer are seen by the hundreds, as well as elk, black bears, otters, beavers and opossums. Wolves find abundant prey, but often at the cost of their lives, because wolf skins are in demand. Game is very common—wild geese, all kinds of wild ducks, swans, quail, woodcocks, rabbits, prairie chickens, turkeys and a stupendous number of wild pigeons.

I have seen birds of rare beauty. Some have plumage of a red fire color, the most vivid possible, with spots of black on the tail and the wings. I have seen others yellow, with tails bigger than their bodies; some sky blue with red breasts; some with markings like great butterflies. I have heard pleasant warbling from all these birds, especially from red birds with large beaks. There are many cranes, both gray and white, that stand taller than a man. The savages value the white cranes for their feathers.

This country is so temperate, so fertile, so beautiful, that it may be called the earthly paradise of North America. It deserves all the care of the king to attract residents to it, so that a solid settlement may be built.

You know that I set out from Montreal on June 2nd, 1701, with 100 men, and I arrived at Detroit on July 24th. First we built Fort Pontchartrain and our houses; then I had some land cleared and wheat sown on October 7th. This wheat, although sown hastily, came up very fine, and was harvested on July 21st. I also had land sown in May with Indian corn, which came up eight feet high. I have a fine garden with vines and fruit trees, and all the soldiers have their own gardens. Next year I will have a mill built, to be absolutely independent of Canada.

Near the fort there is a village of Hurons, to whom I have granted lands in the name of the king, just as I will grant lands to other tribes with permission to settle here. The Hurons have cleared about 200 arpents of land, and will make a great harvest. The Ottawas and the Wolves [Delawares] have settled nearby, and the Miamis have asked for land. Within three miles of the fort there are now four Indian villages with 400 men and their families.

How can these barbarians be made Christians, unless they are made men first? How can they be made men, unless they are humanized and made docile? And how can they be tamed and humanized, except by companionship with a civilized people? You must allow Canadians to settle here, as well as Franciscan priests. It is God's vine. We must cultivate it with many good workers.

Last year my wife and Madame Tonty set out with our families to come to Detroit. Their determination in making so hard a journey was extraordinary. The Iroquois, astonished to see them, kissed their hands and wept for joy, saying that French women had never before come to their country. They said they could no longer doubt the peace we have made with them, as French women come among them with so much confidence. Our own savage allies greeted the women as well, with salutes of musketry. Their arrival proved to the savages that we wished to settle here in earnest, and make it a flourishing settlement.

All this has been done in one year, without costing the king a sou. Monsieur, all is well begun. Finish it, if it please you. Give your orders. I shall carry them out. I have succeeded in what I have tried. If I am not skillful, what matter? I am fortunate. When I succeed, they say it is by a miracle. Again, what matter, as long as I live in a time when miracles are performed?

Your very humble and obedient servant,
La Mothe Cadillac

WAR WITHOUT MERCY

Charles Regnault Dubuisson   1712

In his effort to build a "civilized and humane" settlement at Detroit, Cadillac drew together Indian tribes that were bitter enemies of one another. The Fox Indians in particular were fiercely proud and belligerent. They considered Detroit to be part of their ancestral homeland. By 1712, the Foxes at Detroit were on the verge of warfare with the Ottawas and Hurons. The French commander at Detroit, Charles Dubuisson, took sides against the Foxes, and joined in plotting an attack on their village.

I was told that the Fox and Mascouten nations had received gifts and necklaces from the English, urging those savages to destroy our fort, slaughter us, and slaughter our Indian allies who had settled near us. Those wretches would then withdraw to the English.

In early spring two bands of Fox and Mascouten came to Detroit and encamped within 50 paces of my fort, in spite of my objections. They would not listen to me and spoke most insolently, calling themselves the masters of the land. I had to restrain my speech, for I had only 30 Frenchmen with me. Our Ottawa and Huron allies had not yet returned from their winter hunting grounds. I was constantly exposed to a thousand insults. The Foxes killed our hens, pigeons and other animals, but I dared not say a word. When some of them came into my fort to kill a French settler, I took up arms to resist them, and I forced them to leave.

A Fox named Joseph, who had abandoned his tribe and devoted himself to the French, warned me that the Foxes and Mascoutens planned to burn me in my fort. Hard pressed, I urged my few Frenchmen to bring our corn into the fort promptly. As quickly as possible we pulled down the church, the store house and other buildings outside the fort, to leave a clear field in case we were attacked. We had to skirmish to get stakes, which were outside the fort. I repaired the fort as quickly as possible, using timber we pulled from the houses. I tricked the savages to gain a platform they wanted to keep. I had it set up opposite their fort, with good loop holes, and I had two swivel guns mounted on two great logs to serve as cannon. Yet still I dared not speak my mind to the Foxes, nor refuse to let them enter my fort and trade, for fear they would realize that I knew their wicked plans. I told them that I was repairing my fort because I was afraid of the Miamis. Nevertheless, the Foxes suspected my reasons. I always put a good face on things and encouraged my French, but they believed that they would soon die.

I immediately sent a canoe to the Ottawas and Hurons, to tell them to hurry and join me. I sent another canoe to the far side of the lakes, to warn the Chippewas, Mississagua and Amiquois to join my force. But contrary winds prevented the allied savages from reaching us, which worried me greatly.

The enemies, on their side, were waiting for their allies, the Kickapoos, so they might attack us without fear. The wretches were waiting for the moment when they could set fire to our houses and overwhelm us. It was quite a different matter when they learned that some Mascoutens wintering on St. Joseph River [in northwest Indiana] had been destroyed, to the number of 150 souls, men, women and children, by Ottawas and Potawatomies.

Heaven was watching over us. When I least expected it, a Huron entered my house, quite out of breath, bringing word that 600 warriors would soon arrive—Hurons, Ottawas and Potawatomies—to devour the miserable tribes who had disturbed the peace. The Hurons were highly excited. We had planned this important business all fall and winter, giving presents to our allies. Now the Hurons said it was the will of the French to destroy the Fox and the Mascouten—to annihilate their race.

I realized there was ground for fear in attracting so many tribes to us, not knowing their dispositions. I had the gates of the fort closed. I divided my few Frenchmen into four divisions, each with its commander. I inspected their weapons and prepared ammunition. I posted them on each bastion and put four men in the redoubt. I stationed men at the two curtains, armed with swords fitted to long shafts. I had wedges of iron ready to load into my two cannon. Our reverend father was ready to succor the wounded and to absolve the dying. He prepared the consecrated host. Everything was ready, and we awaited a good fight.

Soon I was told that many people were approaching. I climbed a bastion and, looking toward the woods, I saw an army of nations from the south: the Illinois, the Missouri, the Osage and other tribes still more distant. With them were Ottawas, Potawatomies, Sauks, and Menominees. Detroit has never seen so many people, a whole army, marching in order, with as many flags as there were tribes. I was surprised at how strongly all the tribes were aroused against the Mascoutens and Foxes.

This army made straight for the fort of the Hurons, who told them, "You must not encamp. The matter is too pressing. You must fight for our French father. He loves us. It is just that we should die for him. Ottawas, do you see that smoke? It is three women of your village whom the Foxes are burning."

There was no need to say more. They uttered a great war cry and attacked, with the Hurons and Ottawas at their head. The Foxes and Mascoutens answered with their war cry, and 40 of them came out of their fort, all naked and painted, their arms waving about. They came out to survey our forces and to defy us, to show that they were not afraid, but they were quickly forced to retreat back into their fort.

The chiefs of our allied savages then assembled in the square of my fort to address me. One said, "My father, what you did for us

129

last year, in saving our flesh from the fire when the Foxes wanted to roast it and eat it, deserves that we should bring you our bodies. We do not fear to die for you. We only ask that you have compassion for our wives and our children if we should die, and that you throw a little grass on our bones, to keep away the flies."

I answered them at once. "Thank you, my children. Your offer to die with me gives me great pleasure. I recognize you as the true children of the governor. When you have needs, he will answer them with great zeal. Take courage. Look to your tomahawks, your bows and arrows, and especially your guns. Soon I will give you powder and bullets. Then we will attack."

All the savages gave a great shout of joy, saying, "Our enemies are dead men. Now the sun begins to shine upon us, and the Master of Life takes pity on us." All around the fort the old men made speeches, telling their warriors to obey my commands. I gave them lead and powder. Then all together we shouted the war cry. The very earth trembled with it. The enemy, only a pistol shot away, answered with their war cry. The musket shots began, and the bullets came like hail.

We besieged the enemy for 19 days, firing at them continuously, night and day. To avoid our heavy fire, they dug pits in the ground four or five feet deep. We fired down upon them from two platforms, 20 feet high. They could not get to water, and soon were overwhelmed with hunger and thirst. I had 400 or 500 men surround their fort, day and night, so none could escape and go for help. Our savages scouted the area and brought back prisoners who were coming to join the enemy, not knowing they were besieged. Our savages amused themselves by shooting prisoners and by burning some of them.

The enemy, trying to frighten me, hung red shrouds from their fort. They shouted that they would stain the earth red with our blood. They raised 12 red flags above their village. I viewed these as signs that they were fighting for the English, and in fact, they shouted that their father was English. They shouted to our allies that they would do far better to abandon the French and to join the English. At that, a great war chief of the Potawatomies climbed up on a

130

Fox brave, by George Catlin

platform and shouted back at them: "Wicked tribes, you think you make us afraid with all this red on your fort, but know that if the earth is stained with blood, it will be your own blood. You speak to us of the Englishman, but it is he who causes your loss. He is the evil enemy of prayer, so the Master of Life will punish him, as well as you. You should know that our French father often sends his children against the English to make war, and they bring back so many prisoners they have no place to put them all. The English are cowards who defend themselves deceitfully. They kill men with brandy, a poison drink. We will see what will become of you for listening to the Englishman."

I was obliged to end this conversation when I saw some of the enemy trying to go for water. I knew they were suffering from thirst, so I gave the order to resume fire. Our volley was so heavy we killed more than 30.

Yet every day the enemy killed some of our men. In spite of my efforts, they occupied a house near our fort, and they fired at us from a platform on the roof, protected from our bullets behind its earthen gable. I mounted two mortars on top of a platform, and fired scraps of iron at this gable. With the first two shots, we heard the enemy's platform tumble down, then terrible cries and howls. Some of the enemy were killed.

That evening they asked to speak with us. I called together our allied chiefs, who agreed to let them come, so we could trick them into returning three Ottawa women whom they had taken as prisoners. The next morning we were surprised to see no red flags, but only a single white flag above their village. The great Fox war chief Pemoussa soon entered our fort with two other savages, carrying a white flag. I called together the allied chiefs to meet with him. Here are his words: "My father, I am a dead man. I see clearly that the sky is clear and bright for you, while for me it is all black. By this necklace that I lay at your feet, I ask you to grant two days of peace, so that our old men may hold council and find a way to soften your heart." Then he spoke to the allied chiefs: "This necklace is to beg you to remember that we are your brothers. If you shed our blood, know that it is your blood as well. I beg you to try to soften the heart of our father, whom we have offended. I bring two slaves to replace a little of the blood you may have shed."

I answered him, "If your heart were a little touched, you would have begun by bringing the three women you hold as prisoners. But you have not, and I think your heart is still bad. If you wish me to listen, bring them to me. That is all I have to say."

Two hours later, three chiefs came, flag in hand, with the three women. One chief spoke to us: "My father, here are the three morsels of flesh which you asked for. Now we ask you to make all the tribes depart from here so we may go free to find food for our women and children. Many are dying every day from hunger and thirst. Our whole village repents for having angered you."

I now had the three women, so I no longer cared about humoring them. I replied, "If you had eaten this flesh, you would not be alive now. Our heavy blows would have beaten you deep into the earth. As for the freedom you seek, I will leave it up to my children to answer you. I have no more to say."

A great chief of the Illinois spoke for the allied chiefs: "Hear me, you tribes who have troubled the earth. We see, from all you say, that you are only trying to trick our father again. As soon as we would depart, you would certainly shed his blood. You are dogs that have always bitten the French. You have never been grateful for the benefits you received from the French. So go back to your fort. We will not depart. We wish to die with our father. If he told us to depart, we would not obey him, for we know your evil hearts. Now we will see who is to be master, you or us."

The Fox chiefs returned to their fort, and both sides resumed firing. The enemy sent thick flights of arrows at us—two or three hundred at a time—with lighted fuses of gun powder on them to set fire to our buildings. The arrows caused great trouble as they fell on the straw roofs of our houses. When one house caught fire, the Frenchmen became so frightened they thought they were lost. I said to them, "Come. Take courage. Pull down the straw roofs and replace them with bear and deer skins." Our savages helped us. I ordered two large wooden boats to be brought in and filled with 20 barrels of water. We put wet swabs at the ends of shafts to put out fires quickly, and hooks to pull out arrows.

But my greatest problem was that I no longer had enough food for all my savages. They became discouraged and wanted to leave, some saying that the Fox nation could never be conquered, that the Foxes were braver than any other tribe. (The fickleness of those tribes should teach us that it is dangerous to leave a distant post without French troops.) I soon found myself on the eve of being deserted and left prey to the enemy. The Frenchmen were so scared that they said we should retreat quickly to Mackinac. I replied, "What are you thinking of? Why abandon a post in such a cowardly manner? Drive that thought from your minds, my friends. If you abandon me, the governor general will have you hunted everywhere, and punished for your cowardice. What seems so bad to you? What puts you in such fear? Don't be frightened by what the savages say. I will speak privately to all the chiefs, to put heart in them again. Change your minds. Leave it up to me, and all will go well." They replied that they would not leave without me at their head, and that they would continue to follow my orders. In fact, they have done their duties like brave men.

I then went four days and four nights without sleep, trying to win over the young war chiefs to my cause, convincing them not to depart until our enemies were utterly destroyed. I stripped myself of all that I had to make gifts for them. When I had won over the savages in private, I called a general council. I said to them, "Why is it, when you are on the eve of destroying that wicked tribe, you think of fleeing disgracefully? If you leave now, you will never hold your heads up again. You will always be weighted down with shame. Other tribes will say, 'Those brave warriors fled like cowards and deserted the French.' But take heart. We will find a little food yet. Don't you see that our enemies are holding on by a thread? Hunger and thirst are overpowering them. We shall soon be masters of their lives. You must know that in destroying this tribe, you will give life and peace to your wives and children."

The young war chiefs hardly let me finish, and replied, "Some liar has given you a false report. We are determined to fast still longer.

134

We will not leave you until our enemies have been destroyed." All the old men shouted their approval. They sang and danced the war dance, and many resumed the fight.

Every day a few Sauks, who had been living with the Foxes, came over to us. They told us that the enemy was in a state of utter ruin; that 60 to 80 women and children had died of hunger and thirst; that others were being slain every day; and that they were infected with disease from the bodies of the dead, for they could not bury them because of the heavy fire I kept up constantly.

In this condition, the enemy asked to meet again. We agreed. Four great enemy chiefs—Pemoussa, Allamyma, Kisis and Ouabi-manitou—approached us. Pemoussa had a crown of necklaces on his head, and beaded belts hanging around his body and from his shoulders. He was painted with dark green earth. He was carried by seven women, each painted and bedecked with beads. The other three chiefs carried drums. They marched in order, singing and howling with all their might to the beat of their drums, calling on their demons to have pity on them. They had small figures of demons hanging from their belts.

In the midst of all the allied tribes, Pemoussa then spoke as follows: "I ask you for life. Life is ours no longer. You are the masters of it. All our manitous have deserted us. I bring you my flesh, by the seven slaves that I place at your feet. Do not think that I fear to die. I come only to ask for the lives of our women and children. I beg you to make the sun shine and the sky clear, so we may see the light of day, and do nothing but good in the future. Here are six necklaces which we give to you. These make us your slaves. Take them as a sign that you grant us our lives. My brothers, remember how long you have been of one family with us."

I left it up to our savages to reply, but they had become so enraged that they said nothing. The envoys were sent back without an answer. The poor wretches well knew there was no hope for them. I confess that I was touched with compassion for them, but as war and mercy do not mix, I abandoned them to their sad fate. In fact, I hastened to end the tragedy, so that this example would

135

strike terror into the allies of the English, and into the English themselves.

We began firing again, heavier and heavier. The enemy fought constantly, from within their fort and from outside it, when they ran for water or to snatch a little grass to eat. Their only chance was to get away during a dark night, with rain falling. Such a night came after the 19th day of the siege, and they took advantage of it. They fled at midnight, and we did not learn of it until daybreak.

Our savages pursued them, with Monsieur de Vincennes and several Frenchmen at their head. The enemy stopped on a peninsula near Lake St. Clair, ten miles from the fort. They dug a trench, set up stakes, and laid branches over the top. Some of our men fell into this trap, and more than 20 were killed and wounded. Our men had to encamp and besiege the enemy a second time. The enemy held out for four days longer, fighting with great courage. Finally, unable to fight any more, they surrendered to our people, who showed them no mercy. All were destroyed except women and children, who were taken as slaves, and 150 men who were bound up and brought back to our fort. Our savages amused themselves by shooting four or five of the men every day.

That was the end of those wicked people. Our reverend father celebrated a high mass to give thanks to God for having saved us from the enemy.

The enemy lost a thousand souls—men, women and children.

THE FOX IS IMMORTAL

Gaspard Chaussegros de Lery   1712

*Another account of the battle at Detroit, an account
far more sympathetic to the plight of the Foxes, was
written by Gaspard de Lery, chief engineer of New
France.*

It is well known that when Monsieur Cadillac was
at Detroit, wishing to attract the trade of all the
nations to his post, he sent necklaces to the Mascoutens, Kickapoos and Foxes, asking them to form a village there.
They agreed, and 40 families came to build a fort in the place assigned
to them.

The Fox nation is feared and hated by the other tribes for its
arrogance, so the other tribes began to conspire against the Foxes
who had settled at Detroit. In 1712, when Sieur Dubuisson was
commander at Detroit, 900 Hurons and Ottawas arrived at the French
fort. Dubuisson opened the gate to them, and they quickly entered,
climbed to the bastions overlooking the Fox fort, and fired many
volleys of musket shots at the Foxes.

One of the Fox chiefs then shouted out to the French: "What
does this mean, my father? You asked us to come live near you.
Your message is still fresh in our pouches. Yet now you make war
on us. What cause have we given for this? Have you forgotten that
all the nations you call your children have wet their hands in French

blood? We are the only nation you cannot blame. Now you join our enemies to devour us. But know that the Fox is immortal. Know that if we defend ourselves and shed the blood of Frenchmen, our father cannot blame us."

This speech was cut short by a volley of musketry. The Foxes fired back sharply. Then they worked day and night to dig pits inside their fort to shelter their families from bullets.

On the fourth day the Fox chief, seeing his food and water failing, again called out: "My father, I do not speak to you. I speak to those women who are our enemies, who hide themselves in your fort. Tell them that if they are as brave as they say, they will send out 80 of their best warriors. I will oppose them with only 20 warriors, and if the 80 conquer my men, I will be their slave. But if the 20 overcome their 80, they will be our slaves." The only answer to his speech was a volley of musket shots.

When the 18th day arrived, the Foxes left their fort during the night, undiscovered. They were utterly weak by then, because they had not eaten for 16 days. The next day the men in the French fort were curious when no shots came from the Fox fort. They went to the Fox fort and found no one. The allied chiefs then demanded that the French lead a march in pursuit of the Foxes.

The Foxes fled to a peninsula where they could feed on plants. There they dug a trench which they guarded carefully. Their pursuers soon arrived, closed off the path of escape, and began firing. Sieur de Vincennes asked the Foxes to surrender, and the Fox chief, seeing that he was shut in, called out, "I will surrender myself, but tell me at once, my father, if there is mercy for our women and children. Answer me." Sieur de Vincennes called out that he would grant their lives and safety. But as the Foxes laid down their weapons, they were surrounded in an instant and cut to pieces. Their women and children were made slaves, and most were sold to the French.

Thus perished the Foxes whom Monsieur Cadillac had brought to Detroit. As soon as the Mascoutens and Kickapoos of the large villages learned of this, they sent many war parties into the field— some toward La Baye [Green Bay], others toward Detroit, and others to control the routes of travel. They made all other nations flee.

138

The massacre of the Foxes at Detroit ignited warfare that continued for more than two decades. The surviving Foxes, bent on revenge, harassed French traders throughout the Upper Country.

The French, for their part, tried to annihilate the Fox nation. Time and again, the French and their Indian allies attacked Fox villages: in 1716 at Little Butte des Morts near Green Bay, in 1728 at Green Bay, in 1729 along the Fox River of Wisconsin, in 1730 on the prairie south of Chicago, in 1731 along the Wisconsin River, in 1732 at a lake called Maramech near Chicago, in 1733 at Green Bay, and in 1734 along the Des Moines River.

BETWEEN TWO FIRES

Pierre de Boucherville   1728–29

In 1728 a small army of Frenchmen and allied Indians invaded the Green Bay area to attack a village of Fox Indians. Forewarned of the attack, the Foxes retreated. As they moved westward, the angry Foxes posed a threat to an isolated French fort on the west bank of the Mississippi River at Lake Pepin. The fort's commander, Pierre de Boucherville, recognized the danger, and considered retreating down the Mississippi to reach allied Indians in the Illinois Country. To do so, he and his small band of French soldiers had to pass through the country of their enemies: the Fox, the Mascouten and the Kickapoo.

After Sieur Lignery's expedition against the Foxes had failed, he sent Frenchmen to warn me of all that had happened. I sent six of my men to the Falls of St. Anthony [at the site of Minneapolis] to exhort the Sioux to fight against the Foxes, or at least to refuse them asylum in the Sioux Country. Some days later my men returned to the fort, disappointed with their meeting. The Sioux, after accepting their gifts and amusing them with fine promises, soon showed that they had the hearts of Foxes.

I saw it would be foolhardy to trust in those fickle tribes, so I gathered all our French together on September 18th to decide a course of action. All agreed that the fort could not be held, that our remaining food would not last until the arrival of the convoys, that the fugitive Foxes would try to seduce our allies, and that it was safer to depart at once. So on October 3rd, 12 of us, including Father Guignas, embarked in three canoes. Although the waters of the Mississippi were low, we decided to attempt that route, through enemy country, to reach the Illinois.

As we paddled downstream, we saw signs of the enemy. Hardly had we reached the mouth of the Wisconsin River when we saw traces of a band of Foxes. Three days later we saw their canoes, which they had left at the River of the Iowas [Wapsipinicon River] to penetrate more easily into the surrounding country. Near the River of the Kickapoos [Rock River] we saw camping places and traces of men, women and children. Later we saw animals running along the river bank, seeming to flee from hunters. We saw great fires and heard the sound of guns, which made us believe the enemy was not far off. For greater safety, we traveled by night.

On the morning of October 16th we were discovered by a band of Kickapoos. Leaving their dugout canoes, they ran to their village on a small river 10 miles from the Mississippi. As we approached the mouth of this little river [probably Skunk River of Iowa], we saw savages coming by land and in canoes to bar our way. As we loaded our 25 guns, and resolved to defend ourselves, they called to us from afar, "Brothers. What do you fear? The Foxes are far from here. We are Kickapoos and Mascoutens. We have no evil plans."

They approached and asked that we stay with them a day or two, to trade. In spite of their fine promises, we made ready to proceed. Seeing this, they suddenly surrounded us in 25 dugout canoes, shouting as loud as they could, "Frenchmen, do not resist." Some of them climbed into our canoes. They dragged us to their village, where we thought we would be plundered, or worse; but upon our arrival, far from taking our weapons, they asked us to salute their fort with a volley of musketry. This we did, with fairly good grace.

141

Later they held a council and decided to house us in the lodge of Ouiskouba, whose family had just been killed by French and Illinois. Ouiskouba was away hunting; the Kickapoos sent for him. Our baggage was carried to his lodge, and Father Guignas and I were placed on fine bear-skin mats. We feasted on deer meat. We had no lack of company during the night. Many of the barbarians had never seen a Frenchman, and they came to see us out of curiosity.

The next day some elders entered our lodge and spoke to Father Guignas: "You black gowns [Jesuit priests] once kept peace among the nations. But now you have changed greatly. Not long ago a black gown was seen leading soldiers and waging a bloody war against us." They referred to Father Dumas, the chaplain with Monsieur Desliette's army.

Father Guignas replied, "You do not know the black gowns. It is not our custom to fight and to steep our hands in blood. We follow an army only to help the sick and minister to the dying."

The dispute would have lasted longer, but the young warriors imposed silence on the elders. "Be silent, old babblers," they said. "Are not the French in enough trouble?" These words stopped the insults for a while, but when Father Guignas opened his prayer book, a fresh quarrel broke out. Seeing the red letters in his book, they said, "Those drops of blood warn us to be on guard against this dangerous man." To appease their suspicious minds, the Father closed his book for some days, and we had an interval of peace.

Seven days later, Ouiskouba returned from the hunt. He came to his lodge, and spoke to us as follows: "My father the black gown, and you, my father the French chief, I have just learned that you have been placed in my lodge, and that I shall decide your fate. This is to repay me for the loss of my wife and children, whom the French, acting with the Illinois, have taken from me. Fear not. My heart is good. Our father the governor, whom I saw two years ago, gave me wisdom. His arm governs my thoughts and actions. Rely on my word, and no harm will come to you."

We thanked him and gave him a brasse of tobacco. We promised him that all the good he would do us would be repaid a hundredfold.

142

The next day Chaouenon, a famous Kickapoo speechmaker, visited me. I said to him, "I know your face. Did I not see you at Detroit in Cadillac's time? You were then considered a wise man, and I am delighted to see you." The savage was charmed by my compliment and was pleased with the tobacco I gave him. He advised me to be wise, and to get out of trouble cleverly by giving presents to the young men of the tribe.

I asked that a council be assembled, where I gave them four barrels of gun powder, two guns, a 30-pound kettle, seven pounds of vermilion, 12 hatchets, two dozen large knives, seven braided coats, two cloth blankets, two white blankets, and seven bags of shot. I addressed them, saying, "My brothers, children of the governor: I have learned that the French and their allies have driven the Foxes from their country to punish them for having deluged the earth with blood, and for reddening the waters of the Mississippi with the blood of Frenchmen. Perfidious people that they are, when we passed through their land a year ago, they promised to remain at peace and to atone for the past. We told them they could hope for clemency from the governor, and we would strive to pacify the land and urge the Sioux to peace. I have kept my word, and have stopped several bands of Chippewas, and of Sioux, who breathed nothing but war. Now I have left my fort to inform our father, the governor, of all this, and to learn his intentions. Today, by these gifts, I ask you that my path be made clear. I have reason to fear the Fox, for I know he is not far from here. He would bring trouble to you as well as to us, were he to take it into his head to come to this village. I beg you, Kickapoos and Mascoutens, make our path clear. Do not refuse so reasonable a request."

They replied that our gifts would be set aside for the night, and they would answer us the following day.

The next day a great council was held. A savage slave, seven or eight years old, was placed on a white beaver robe. The child, along with some dried beaver meat, was offered as a gift to us. A Kickapoo chief spoke: "To our father, the governor, we offer our words, this little slave, and this beaver flesh, to beg the governor not to be angry with us if we keep the French chief, the black gown and their companions. After the flight of the Foxes, the burning of their lodges, and the ravaging of their fields, we were warned to withdraw to the banks of the Mississippi River, because our father the governor was angry with us. We were warned that all the nations that spend the winter near us would soon attack us. So now we stop you, Frenchmen, to save our children's lives. You will be our safeguard. You say you fear the Foxes! My brothers, what have you to fear? The Foxes are far from here. Even if they come for you, they will not succeed. Look at these warriors, all brave young men who surround you. All promise to die with you. Their bodies will serve as your ramparts. So, Frenchmen, prepare to spend the winter with us. Begin to build cabins."

I replied to him, "Have you thought well about what I said yesterday? Do you realize that you will have to answer for us, body for body? Do you know that if any accident should befall us, you will be held accountable?"

"We know it," he answered. "We think of it. We have decided after much thought."

So we attacked the forest with our axes, and with the help of the young Kickapoos, we finished our cabins in a week.

Just as we were beginning to settle down and live on good terms, a Kickapoo one day came to my cabin to warn me that ten Foxes had arrived in the village. A moment later, Kansekoe, chief of the Foxes, entered my cabin, held out his hand to me and said, "I greet you, my father." To deceive me, he said he had been told to lodge in my cabin. I put a good face on the situation, in spite of my surprise, and I offered food to my treacherous visitor.

Our faithful Chaouenon later told me that Kansekoe was trying to seduce the Kickapoos with gifts. Fortunately, I had already won over the young Kickapoos with gifts of my own. Although the Kickapoos were intimidated by threats from the Foxes, the Kickapoos refused a pipe of war and a necklace of wampum beads that the Foxes offered them. The Foxes angrily departed, and I immediately urged the young Kickapoos to move their camp to a nearby island, less exposed to attack by the Foxes.

About this time we learned of a barbaric plan of Pechicamengoa, a Kickapoo chief and a dreaded warrior, who had many relatives and young Kickapoos at his command. He was married to a Fox wife, so the Foxes had no trouble convincing him to kill Father Guignas. They told Pechicamengoa that he should not come to their village without the good father's scalp. This chief hid his wicked plan for some days, so he would not fail in striking his blow. One fine night he invited two of his young men to join him in a sweat lodge, not so much to sweat, as to allow his secret to ooze out and to induce the young men to help him. But God did not permit him to succeed. Once the sweating was over, the young Kickapoos indignantly told the friendly chiefs about this treachery. "What!" they exclaimed. "We thought we had only the Foxes to fear. Now our own brother betrays us and wishes to stain our mats with blood, by massacring the French! If a Fox would have tried to take the father's life, we would have settled the matter by breaking his head. But the guilty man is a chief of our nation! Let us try to calm him with gifts." They offered him gifts, and he accepted, promising to forget his cowardly plan. After that, ten Kickapoos watched over our safety night and day.

But we soon learned of another threat, for Kansekoe and the other nine Foxes had met 30 Foxes. All were now coming for us. They had orders to threaten the Kickapoos with the arrival of 600 warriors, both Fox and Winnebago, who supposedly were coming to be revenged for past insults. When the 40 Foxes arrived, the Kickapoos allowed them onto the island, but they also reinforced the guard watching over our safety.

On entering the village, a Fox made this speech: "We are sad, my brothers. We have been driven from our lands by the French. Our sorrow has brought us here, to beg you to wipe away our tears. You are our relatives. Do not refuse what we ask. Give us as many Frenchmen as you choose. We do not demand them all."

They went to the lodge of our friend Chaouenon, convinced that if they could win him over, the other chiefs would agree. The Fox savages began to weep for their dead, making the air resound with their cries. They spread out a bloody robe, a shell red with

145

Fox and Sauk Indians, by Carl Bodmer

blood, and a sacred pipe with feathers dripping blood. All this blood called most eloquently for our own. A tall, young Fox warrior, covered with paint, then arose, lit his war pipe, and presented it to Chaouenon and to the Kickapoo chiefs. The young chiefs barely touched it with their lips, and drew but a puff or two, but the old chiefs smoked heartily and emptied the Fox's war pipe, to show they agreed with him. The Kickapoos then told the Foxes they would answer the next day. The young Kickapoos passed that whole night without sleep, as the Foxes roamed about endlessly, making great threats.

The next day a Kickapoo gave their answer: "My brothers, you know that we have no evil plan in stopping the French. We wish them to live. What would become of us, if they died while in our hands? My brothers, leave us in peace. Accept our gift, for we will die rather than give up a single Frenchman."

The Foxes, angered at this reply, arose with fire in their eyes. They threatened revenge, made up their bundles, and departed. After a three-day journey, they met a Kickapoo and a Mascouten, whom they massacred without pity, and carried the scalps home with them. This murder greatly alarmed the other Foxes. The old men cried, "We are lost beyond hope! You foolish young men, it must be a slight thing in your eyes to rise up against all the nations who have sworn to destroy us. Now you must massacre our kinsmen as well! What will we do to atone for this murder?"

They at once sent five men to go and weep for the two dead, and to offer their lives to an old Kickapoo who was not far from the Fox village. As they approached him, they spread out a white robe, on which two Foxes stretched themselves, quite naked. "Revenge yourself, my brother," they said. "Your children have been killed, so we offer you our bodies. Vent your rage on us."

The old man answered, "Our village soon will learn of your crime. The matter is no longer in my hands. The young Kickapoo chiefs will decide." At this, the Foxes arose and returned home.

Soon afterward, two young Kickapoos arrived on the bank of the river near the Kickapoo village. They uttered death yells in the night. A dug-out canoe was sent for them, and they told of the sad

147

event. Their word spread dismay throughout the village. Nothing was heard but weeping and horrible yells. At once messengers were sent into the woods with the warning that all Kickapoos should take refuge on the island. The old men came to me, and blamed me for the deaths of their young men. "You are the cause of this murder," they said, "and we are paying dearly for having you."

I replied, "If you had believed me and agreed to let us pass, this would not have happened. Did I not warn you?"

"You are right," they said. "But what can we do now? We are between two fires. The Fox has killed us. The Illinois has killed us. The Frenchman is angry with us. What are we to do?"

I replied, "I can help you arrange your affairs. Send two chiefs with me, and I will start for the Illinois Country, where I promise to help you make peace with those tribes."

To this they agreed.

> *De Boucherville soon succeeded in drawing the Kickapoos into an alliance with the Illinois and with the French. He urged the Kickapoos to join in destroying their kinsmen, the Foxes.*
>
> *The governor of New France wrote to the Kickapoos: "If the Foxes have killed you, you see they are no longer your kin. I urge you to avenge yourselves. That wicked nation can live no longer. The king wishes their death."*

TO DESTROY A NATION

Charles de Beauharnois   1733

In the year 1733, Charles de Beauharnois, governor of New France, confidently assured the king's minister that the Fox nation would soon be annihilated. Part of his letter follows.

The Foxes have at last abandoned their fort. Only 40 warriors and 10 boys remain among them. They have gone to La Baye [Green Bay] to beg the Sieur de Villiers for mercy. He has brought four of their most important men here to Montreal. I am sending de Villiers back immediately with orders to bring all the Foxes to Montreal, or to destroy them. If he succeeds in bringing them here, we should send them to France as slaves, to be distributed among the islands of the West Indies. If we only disperse them among our villages of settled savages, they might desert to the English.

If the wretched remnant of that nation will not obey, the Sieur de Villiers has orders to kill them, without thinking of taking a prisoner, so as not to leave a single one of that race alive in the Upper Country.

I remain, with very profound respect, your very humble and very obedient servant,

Beauharnois

149

De Villiers soon returned to Green Bay like a conquering hero, at the head of 80 Frenchmen and 250 allied Indians. He expected to sweep away the last of the Fox nation, once and for all. The surprising results of his expedition were related four months later, in another letter from Governor Beauharnois to the French ministry.

I informed you in my last letter of the orders I had given to the Sieur de Villiers regarding treatment of the Foxes. The result has not fulfilled my expectations.

The Sieur de Villiers arrived at his fort at Green Bay on September 16th, where he left a force of 60 French and 200 savages—Ottawas, Menominees and Chippewas—a mile away, giving them orders to march as soon as they heard three gunshots. He also sent his son, an ensign, with 10 French and 50 savages, to Le Petit Cacalin [the site of Kaukauna, Wisconsin] to block the Foxes' route of escape.

The last of the Foxes were living with the Sauks in their fort at Green Bay. When de Villiers arrived, he sent at once for the Sauk chiefs. They came to him, and he explained that the governor would grant the last of the Foxes their lives, if they would submit to his orders and go to Montreal. When the Sauk chiefs made no firm answer, de Villiers sent them back to their fort to tell their tribe that if they did not send out the Foxes within a certain time, he would go and seize the Foxes. When the time had passed and no Foxes appeared, de Villiers went to the Sauk fort himself with two of his sons, his son-in-law, and seven or eight other French. He ordered the rest of the French to guard the approaches to the fort, to keep the Foxes from escaping.

As de Villiers arrived at the fort, he was met at the gate by armed Sauks. When he asked the Sauks to turn over the Foxes, they told him to leave. He tried to force his way into the fort, and a Sauk approached him with raised tomahawk. Suddenly three shots were fired, one killing de Villiers' son who stood by his side. The father and the other French then fired their pieces, and the Sauks returned fire, killing the Sieur de Villiers himself, and wounding three French.

150

The other French immediately ran toward the fort, but the Sauks made a sortie against them, killing eight French. Our allied savages, who had remained in the French fort, now ran to assist the others. The Sauks, seeing them coming, withdrew into their fort. Three of the Sauks were killed.

After a siege of three days, the Sauks and the last of the Foxes left their fort in the dead of night. The younger de Villiers, returning from Le Petit Cacalin, quickly assembled all the French and savages, pursued the Sauks, and overtook them by late afternoon [near the site of Menasha, Wisconsin]. He attacked and fought them until nightfall. Two French were killed and 12 wounded. Twenty Sauks and six Foxes were killed in this fight. Among our allies, the Ottawas lost nine men, including their grand chief; the Menominees six; the Chippewas two.

I will at once give orders to attack the Sauks and the remaining Foxes, to avenge the French blood that has been lost.

I remain, with very profound respect, your very humble and very obedient servant,

Beauharnois

The battle at Green Bay was a fiasco for the French. Instead of crushing the Fox nation, the French provoked a new enemy alliance between the Foxes and the Sauks. The battle demonstrated to other natives that the French could be defeated. Some tribes freed their Fox prisoners, who returned to reinforce that nation. Some tribes refused to attack the Foxes. Some sent ambassadors to Montreal to plead for peace with the Foxes.

Governor Beauharnois remarked, "The savages have their policy, as we have ours. They are not pleased at seeing a nation destroyed, for fear that their turn may come."

New France finally made peace with the Foxes in 1734, ending hostilities that had lasted for more than two decades.

151

A STORM
ABOUT TO BURST

Charles de Longueuil   1752

*In the 1740's, English fur traders began to challenge
French influence over the natives of the Upper Country.
The English directed their challenge from a wilderness
outpost they called Pickawillany (on the banks of the
Miami River, north of the present site of Cincinnati).
There they conspired with a Miami chief, whom the
French derisively called "La Demoiselle." By 1752
Charles de Longueuil, governor of New France, feared
a widespread revolt against the French. He expressed
his fears in a letter to the king's minister.*

You already know that the followers of the Miami
chief La Demoiselle have pushed their rebellion
to excess, have adopted the English, and have
openly declared themselves the sworn enemies of the French. You
also know that I have ordered Monsieur de Celeron to capture La
Demoiselle's fort, to expel the English from La Belle Riviere [Ohio
River], to punish the rebel nations, and to make them feel the king's
power.

In fact, my orders were not executed. I cannot fathom the reasons
why Monsieur de Celeron could not obey them. He reports that
after 20 days of council with the allied savages at Detroit, they have
decided that the French militia is too small to attack La Demoiselle.

152

They have decided to hold the hatchet until spring, when success will be certain. Their delay put it out of his power to do anything with the few Frenchmen he had. He advises us not to depend on the savages for any expedition. In his last letter, he states that he cannot say anything certain about the savages at Detroit, since they have departed for their winter hunting grounds.

The commander at Fort of the Miamis [on the Maumee River] has failed to bring the loyal Miamis back from White River. Smallpox has made all of them flee. Many of our most trusted savages have died of it. The commander at the River St. Joseph reports that all nations seem to take sides against us. The nations at Missilimakina [Mackinac] have not budged to help us. Some of the enemy have been seen on the Grand River. It is likely that the commander at Fort Chartres [on the Mississippi River] is losing authority over the Illinois tribes.

The commander at Vincennes [on the Wabash River] reports that we must use all means to protect ourselves from the storm about to burst upon the French. He is busy securing himself against the fury of our enemies.

On the other hand, all the savages of the Ohio River are for the English. They all are resolved to sustain each other, and every band of savages that goes there adds to the rebel forces.

The commanders at our posts have much more cause to be on their guard, since our enemies have steeped their hands in French blood. The Nipissings have taken two scalps near La Demoiselle's village. The Miamis of Rock River have scalped two soldiers. The Piankashaws have killed nine Frenchmen and two slaves, after four of their nation were killed by Frenchmen. The English are the indirect authors of the murders of the French. They have paid the Miamis for the scalps of the two French soldiers.

This spring I expect to receive word that other Frenchmen have been killed. I have heard that the Illinois, Iowa, Piankashaw, Miami, Delaware, Shawnee and the Five Nations [Iroquois] will meet this year at La Demoiselle's fort. It all tends to a general revolt.

Added to our troubles is the shortage of food and the threat of famine at our southern posts. The crops have failed at Detroit, the

153

Illinois Country, and the Ohio River. In those places Frenchmen eat only two handfuls of Indian corn a day, without meat, grease or salt. Famine is not the only scourge we suffer. Smallpox commits ravages. It prevails on the Ohio River. It begins to reach Detroit. If it would only break out and spread among the rebels, it would serve us as well as an army.

You see, Monsieur, the sorrowful condition of the entire Upper Country.

I am with most profound respect, Monsieur, your most humble and most obedient servant.

Longueuil

The French soon were delivered from their plight by a young "half-breed" army cadet at Mackinac. He was Charles de Langlade, son of a French fur trader and his Ottawa Indian wife. At age 23, Langlade inspired 240 of his Ottawa kinsmen to march against the rebel outpost at Pickawillany. They took the fort by surprise, killed La Demoiselle, captured a fortune in English trade goods, and forced the English traders to retire to Pennsylvania. Pickawillany was abandoned.

Langlade's raid set in motion the military forces of France and England alike. Two years later, they clashed at Fort Duquesne, the first major battle of the French and Indian War.

HALF-BREED WARRIOR

Augustin Grignon   1754–61

When France went to war with England in 1754, the prize at stake was control of much of North America. France called upon Charles de Langlade, the young "half-breed" soldier from Mackinac, to lead Upper Country Indians into battle against the English. During seven long years of warfare, Langlade repeatedly inspired the natives to fight for the French. But Langlade left no personal record of his service. The following account was related years later by Langlade's grandson, Augustin Grignon, who, as a boy, had listened to his grandfather's recollections.

My grandfather, Charles de Langlade, was born in 1729 in an Ottawa village near Mackinac, the son of a French fur trader and his Ottawa wife, sister of Chief Nissowaquet. The young Charles was educated by French missionaries at Mackinac.

When he was ten years old, the Ottawas were fighting a war against a southern tribe allied with the English. The enemy's fort was located on a prairie. Twice the Ottawas had attacked the place, and twice they had been defeated. When urged by the French commander to make a third attempt on the enemy's stronghold, the Ottawas refused. At last, Chief Nissowaquet and his brothers, prompted by a superstitious dream, said they would attack again, but only if accompanied by their young nephew, Charles de Langlade.

The commander went to Charles' father and told him of the Ottawas' requirement. Surprised at the request for a mere lad to accompany a war party, Monsieur de Langlade asked his son whether the plan was his idea. When Charles said it was not, the father said, "Well, you must go with your uncles. But never let me hear of you being a coward."

The Ottawa war party left with young Charles. When they reached the enemy village, they placed the boy to the rear, in full view of the battle. After a heavy attack, the place was taken. Charles used to say that, in watching the battle from a distance, it seemed like a game of ball. After that, whenever the Ottawas went to war, they were accompanied by young Charles de Langlade.

The French and Indian War broke out in 1754, when Charles was but 25 years old, full of youth and vigor. The war opened a new field for his enterprising spirit. Such was the reputation of Charles de Langlade, his long experience in frontier service, and his great influence over the powerful Ottawas and other tribes, that he was pointed out at once to the governor-general of New France as admirably suited to lead the border French and the Indians of the Upper Country in the terrible war about to begin.

His first service in the war was to raise the tribes of the Upper Country—Ottawa, Chippewa, Menominee, Winnebago, Potawatomi, Huron, and perhaps others—and to lead them to Fort Duquesue [at the site of Pittsburgh, Pennsylvania], to defend it against the English. This was in 1755. About 1,500 French and Indians were there, and Charles de Langlade commanded almost all the Indians.

When Langlade arrived at the fort, he sent out spies. They soon returned with word that a large English army under General Braddock was within a half day's march of the Monangahela River, cutting a road as it advanced. It was decided that Monsieur Beaujeu, with what French could be spared, and with the Indian force under Langlade, should advance to the Monongahela and attack the English as they crossed the river. The English arrived at the river about noon, halted, and prepared for dinner, while the French and Indians hid on the other shore. Langlade then went to Beaujeu and said no time should be lost. The attack should start at once. Beaujeu made no reply. Langlade then called the chiefs together and told them to demand orders to attack. Again Beaujeu did not reply. Langlade again went to Beaujeu and said, "If you do not intend to fight at all, then it is well to act as you do. But if we are to fight, now is the time, while the English are eating or crossing the river. Such an opportunity will not occur again. The English are too powerful to be met in open battle."

Beaujeu was disheartened, seeing the strength of the English. He seemed in great doubt what to do. At last he gave orders to attack. The attack was commenced at once. The English, taken completely by surprise, had to rush into battle. English officers, who had their napkins pinned to their breasts, quickly seized their weapons and took part. A good many were killed with napkins still pinned on their coats. The English fought from lower ground and over-shot the French. Their cannon balls struck the trees half-way up, among the branches. French and Indian losses were very small. Most who were killed or injured were not struck by enemy bullets, but by falling limbs cut from the trees by the over-shooting of the English cannon. Beaujeu was one of those killed.

The English were defeated and driven back with heavy losses.

Langlade's first order after the battle was to search the immense supplies the English had abandoned, and to pour all liquor upon the ground. He did not want the Indians to drink so freely as to render them dangerous to the French and to each other. The Indians watched with sorrow at this waste, but they did not interfere with the orders of their honored leader. The Indians, as well as many French, found enough excitement in stripping the bodies of the slain. Most of the British officers were superbly clothed, because this was their first campaign since arriving from England. Their clothing and equipment were objects of great interest and value.

I do not know whether my grandfather returned home or remained at Fort Duquesne after Braddock's defeat. I do know that in August, 1756, he was ordered to strike at Ford Cumberland, and to discover whether the English were moving toward the Ohio River.

Battle at Fort Duquesne, by Edwin Deming

In 1757 Langlade served under General Montcalm in the capture of Fort William Henry. At the close of that campaign, he returned to Mackinac as second in command.

The next year Langlade again wended his way eastward, at the head of a French and Indian force, sharing the dangers and services of that hard campaign. We can scarcely realize the hardships of their service, marching thousands of miles through a wilderness country, relying on wild game for food.

It is remarkable that Langlade could have convinced so many Indians of different tribes to leave their villages and to make the long journey eastward, to fight against the English. He once told me how he enlisted a band of reluctant Potawatomies, then living at Milwaukee River. He spoke to them awhile, but could not persuade them; so he resorted to his knowledge of Indian customs. He killed several dogs, and prepared for the "Feast of the Dog" by placing the raw heart of a dog on each of two stakes. As the Indians ate, Langlade sang the war song and danced around the stakes. As he passed each stake, he bent down and took a bite of the raw heart. This was an appeal to Indian bravery, signifying that if they too had brave hearts, they would follow Langlade's example and go with him to war. The Potawatomies could not resist this ancient custom. One after another they joined in the war song and tasted the dogs' hearts, until all had become followers of Langlade.

Amable de Gere used to tell me that he never saw so cool and fearless a man in battle as Charles de Langlade. In one battle he saw my grandfather—while waiting for his gun to cool—draw his pipe from his pouch, cut his tobacco, fill his pipe, take a piece of punk wood, strike fire, and smoke his pipe, as calmly as though he was at his own fireside. Having cooled his gun and refreshed himself, he resumed his part in the battle.

I know that Charles de Langlade fought in the great battle on the Plains of Abraham, before Quebec, where General Montcalm was killed. Langlade's two brothers were also killed in that desperate conflict. When the battle was over and the surviving French commander surrendered Quebec, Langlade left the place in disgust, with his chosen followers.

159

Early the next year, 1760, Langlade again led French and Indians to war. That year's campaign must have been severe, as they opposed a far superior English force.

On September 9th, 1760, Langlade received word from Governor Vaudreuil that he had been compelled to surrender all Canada to the British. The governor wrote, "You will assemble all the officers and soldiers at Mackinac, make them lay down their arms, and accompany them to a seaport convenient for their departure to France. You will send a copy of this letter to St. Joseph and the other posts of the Upper Country, presuming some soldiers may be there. I hope to have the pleasure of seeing you in France."

> *Charles de Langlade, the half-breed frontiersman, never left for France. Instead, he lived under British rule at Mackinac for several years, then moved his family to Green Bay, where he helped establish a permanent settlement. Many other French Canadians, like Langlade, stayed on in the wilderness. The Upper Country had become their home.*

160

A STRANGER TO THE TRADE

Alexander Henry   1761

When Canada fell to England in 1760, a few brave Englishmen promptly set off for the Upper Country, hoping to enter the fur trade, and to build their fortunes. Perhaps the most unlikely of them was young Alexander Henry. At age 21, Henry knew nothing about the Upper Country or its natives. He had never used showshoes, nor even paddled a canoe. Nevertheless, just a few months after the final battle of the French and Indian War, Henry outfitted several trade canoes, employed a crew of French Canadians, and boldly set off for the northwest wilderness. At the time, he did not realize that Indians of the Upper Country still considered themselves to be at war with the English.

The French surrender of Montreal, and with it the surrender of all Canada, threw open a vast new market to British adventure. At that time there were no goods in Montreal for the Indian trade, so I went to Albany to buy merchandise, returning to Montreal on June 15th, 1761. I was a complete stranger to the fur trade, so I relied on the advice of a French assistant, one Etienne Campion.

The canoes I provided for the Indian trade were 32 feet in length and 4½ feet in greatest width, made of birch bark a quarter of an inch thick, lined with small splints, and further strengthened by ribs of cedar wood. Small roots of the spruce tree provided wattap, with which the bark was sewn. The gum of the pine tree took the place of tar. Such a canoe could carry more than four tons of freight, yet was so light when empty that it could be carried by four men. I hired eight French Canadians for each canoe, placing skilled men, at double the wages of the rest, in the bow and stern.

A voyage to the Upper Country is said to begin at the Rapids of Saint Anne, near the Island of Montreal. There the men go to confession and offer up their vows, for Saint Anne is the patroness of Canadians in all their travels by water. Another custom observed at Saint Anne's is the distribution of a gallon of rum to each man, for use during the voyage. It is likewise their custom to drink all of the liquor on the spot. No sooner were the saint and the priest dismissed, than the drinking began. My men surpassed even drunken Indians in singing, fighting and savage gestures. The next morning we reloaded our canoes and pursued our journey.

Our voyage from Montreal to Michilimackinak [Mackinac] followed the Ottawa River, Lake Nippissing and the French River—a route shorter for canoes than following Lake Ontario and Lake Erie. While paddling up the Ottawa River we met several canoes of Indians, and I bought from them maple sugar and beaver skins. Before they left us, they asked my men whether I was an Englishman. When told I was, they said I must be mad in my pursuit of beaver skins, to risk my life so. They said, "The Upper Indians will surely kill him," meaning myself. I was the first Englishman those Indians had ever met.

On the 31st day of August, we reached the mouth of the French River. There I first saw the billows of Lake Huron, which lay stretched across the horizon like an ocean. As we entered the lake, the waves ran high from the south, breaking over the rocks. At first I was alarmed, but the canoes rode on the water with the ease of sea birds.

The next day we reached a large village of Ottawa Indians on an island called La Cloche. At first the Ottawas were civil and kind. I traded small articles for fish and dried meat, and they remained friendly until they learned I was an Englishman. Then they told my

162

men that the Indians at Mackinac would surely kill me, so they had a right to share in the plunder. They demanded a keg of rum, and I agreed, on the condition they not molest me. The repeated warnings of sure death at Mackinac burdened my thoughts, yet I could no longer return to Montreal, for my food was almost gone.

I noticed that the Indians seemed to be hostile only against the English. There was the most cordial good will between them and my French Canadian assistants. This suggested one means of escape— to dress like a Canadian in the trade and to imitate, as best I could, their appearance and manners. I laid aside my English clothes and covered myself with a cloth about the waist, a shirt hanging loose, a blanket coat, and a red, woolen hat. Next I smeared my face and hands with dirt and grease. This done, I took the place of one of my men. When Indians approached, I used the paddle with as much skill as I could muster. In this disguise I reached Mackinac Island, where there was a Chippewa village of 100 warriors. As the Chippewas asked us for news, I feared discovery, particularly when they asked whether any Englishmen were coming to Mackinac. One of them, in fact, looked at me, laughed, and pointed me out to another. Yet without suspecting me to be English, they let me pass.

Leaving Mackinac Island as speedily as possible, I crossed the strait, and landed at the fort at Mackinac. This fort stands on the south side of the strait, which joins Lake Huron and Lake Michigan. The fort covers two acres, and is enclosed with cedar stakes. It is so close to the water that when the wind is high from the west, the waves break against the stockade. On the bastions are two small English cannon, captured some years before by Canadians who had plundered British posts on Hudson's Bay.

Here I gave charge of my property to my assistant, Campion, who agreed that he would act as owner. My men were told to hide the fact that I was an Englishman, but they soon betrayed my secret, and I was visited by the French Canadian inhabitants. With a great show of civility, they assured me that I could not stay at Mackinac without immediate risk. They suggested that I lose no time in escaping to Detroit. Campion told me later that he believed the Canadian inhabitants of the fort were more hostile than the Indians, because

163

they were jealous of English traders penetrating into their country. Most of them had served in the French army.

Soon afterward, I was warned that Chippewa warriors from the island were on their way to pay me a visit. In a short time they appeared at my house, about 60 in number, led by Minavavana, their chief. They walked in single file, each with a tomahawk in one hand and a scalping knife in the other. Their bodies were naked from the waist up; a few had blankets thrown over their shoulders. Their faces were painted black with charcoal worked up with grease. Their bodies were painted with clay, in fanciful patterns. Some had feathers on their heads or through their noses. What sensations I had, as I watched the approach of this frightful band!

The chief entered first. The rest followed silently. The chief made a sign. They seated themselves on the floor.

Minavavana was about 50 years old, and six feet tall. His face showed an indescribable mixture of good and evil. He looked steadfastly at me as he talked with Campion, asking how long it had been since I left Montreal. He said the English seem to be brave men, not afraid of death, since they dare to go alone among their enemies.

The Indians gravely smoked their pipes, and I endured the torments of suspense. At last Minavavana took a few necklaces in his hand, and made the following speech:

"Englishman, it is to you that I speak, and I demand your attention!

"Englishman, you know that the French king is our father. He promised to be such. We, in return, promised to be his children. This promise we have kept.

"Englishman, it is you who have made war with our father. You are his enemy. How could you have the boldness to venture among us, his children?

"Englishman, we are told that our father, the King of France, is old and weak; that he has fallen asleep, tired of making war upon your nation. During his sleep, you have taken advantage of him, and have taken Canada for yourselves. But his nap has almost ended. I think I hear him stirring, asking for his children, the Indians. When he awakens, what must become of you? He will destroy you utterly!

164

"Englishman, although you have conquered the French, you have not conquered us! We are not your slaves. These lakes, these woods and mountains were left to us by our ancestors. These are our inheritance. We will give them to no one. Your nation supposes that we, like the white people, cannot live without bread and pork and beef. You should know that the Great Spirit and Master of Life has provided food for us always, in these vast lakes and on these wooded mountains.

"Englishman, our father, the King of France, asked our young men to make war upon your nation. In this warfare, many of our young men have been killed. It is our custom to retaliate, so that the spirits of the slain are satisfied.

"Englishman, as for you, we consider that you have risked your life among us, expecting that we would not harm you. You do not come armed, to make war. You come in peace, to trade with us, and to supply our needs. We shall regard you as a brother. You may sleep peacefully, without fear of the Chippewas. As a token of our friendship, we give you this pipe to smoke."

I then replied to Minavavana, declaring that the King of France had surrendered Canada to the King of England, whom they should now regard as their father. I said that I had come to furnish them with merchandise.

Several days later, 300 British troops marched into the fort, dispelling all my fears.

PONTIAC'S REBELLION

Anonymous   1763

The victorious British thought they could control the Upper Country by military force alone. They occupied forts throughout the wilderness, yet failed to make real peace with the Indians. English soldiers often were contemptuous of the Indians. English trade goods were expensive. Ammunition, much needed by the Indians, was not available. So hatred for the English festered among the natives of the Upper Country. One Indian, an Ottawa chief named Pontiac, tried to unite the Indian nations for a single assault against the English. Chief Pontiac's call to arms at Detroit was recorded by an anonymous French author.

Pontiac was the great leader of the Ottawas, Chippewas, Potawatomies, and all the nations of the lakes and rivers of the north. He believed that none but those nations should live on this part of the earth, and he resolved to annihilate the English. He enlisted his own nation, the Ottawas, then he tried to draw the Potawatomies and the Hurons to his cause, by calling them to a council held near Detroit, [in April, 1763]. In council he stood before them and showed them war belts which he pretended to have received from the King of France, urging an onslaught upon the English.

To win the nations over, Pontiac told them about a prophet among the Wolf [Delaware] Indians who had been in heaven and who had seen the Master of Life. Pontiac told the story as follows: The Delaware prophet, wanting to see the "Master of Life," as all Indians call the good God, decided to undertake the journey to paradise. Not knowing anyone who had been to heaven who could show him the way, he began to conjure and to dream. In his dream he imagined that he only had to begin his journey, and he soon would reach heaven. Very early the next morning he left his lodge, equipped as a hunter. On the eighth day of his journey at sunset, he stopped to make camp on the bank of a brook, next to a small prairie. As he prepared his lodge and lit a fire, he noticed three wide, well-beaten paths on the far side of the prairie. As night grew darker, the paths grew more distinct. The Indian was surprised and frightened, but he remembered his dream, and he believed that one of the paths might lead him to heaven.

The next morning he began to follow the widest path, but at mid-day a great fire suddenly flared up from the ground. He turned back and started to follow the widest of the other two paths, but on it he again saw a fire coming from the ground. He then retraced his steps to the third path, which he followed for a whole day.

All at once a splendidly white mountain appeared before him, and upon the mountain sat a woman with dazzling beauty and garments whiter than snow. She said to him, "I know you have come to speak with the Master of Life. To see him, you must remove all your clothing and wash yourself in the river. Then you must climb this mountain, using only your left hand and left foot."

The mountain was steep and smooth, yet after much trouble he climbed to the top. There he saw three villages, much more beautiful than his own, and he walked toward the most beautiful. At the gate he was met by a handsome man, all dressed in white, who took him by the hand. He was led to a place of great beauty. There he saw the Master of Life, who took him by the hand and told him to be seated.

God then said to him, "I am the Master of Life. Listen to what I will tell you, for yourself and for all Indians. I am the maker of heaven and earth—trees, lakes, rivers, men, all that you see. Because I love you, you must do my will. You must avoid that which I hate.

167

I hate for you to drink until you lose your reason. I hate that you take two wives, or run after the wives of others. I hate that you fight each other. When you go to war, you conjure and you sing the medicine song, thinking that you speak to me. You only deceive yourselves. It is to the Manitou that you speak. He is a wicked spirit who induces you to evil. For want of knowing me, you listen to him. The land on which you dwell I made for you, not for others. Why do you suffer the whites to dwell upon your lands? Can you not do without them? I know that those whom you call the children of your great father [the French] have supplied your needs. But if you were not wicked, you would not need them. You could live as you did before you knew them. Before they arrived, your bow and arrow sustained you. You needed no gun, no powder. The flesh of animals was your food, their skins your clothing. When I saw you inclined to evil, I sent the animals into the depths of the forest. Become good again and do my will, and I will send the animals to you. Drive away those dogs in red clothing [British soldiers] who come to trouble your lands. Drive them away. Make war against them. I love them not. They know me not. They are my enemies. Send them back to the lands I have made for them. Let them remain there."

The prophet then promised to do the will of the Master of Life, and to urge all Indians to do the same. Word of this prophet's adventure spread from village to village until it reached Pontiac, who believed it as an article of faith. He instilled it into the spirits of all those who listened to him, as an oracle. Those who listened said Pontiac had only to speak, and they would follow him.

The speech, which Pontiac delivered in such an energetic tone, produced its desired effect upon members of the council. They all swore the complete destruction of the English. It was decided that Pontiac, at the head of 60 chosen men, would go to the fort [at Detroit] to ask the English commander for a grand council; that they would have weapons hidden under their blankets; and that the rest of the village, armed with tomahawks, dirks and knives—also hidden under their blankets—would follow them and enter the fort. The Ottawa women were to enter as well, furnished with shortened guns and other weapons. They were to take up their position in the rear streets of the fort, and await the signal, which would be a war-cry given by the great Chief Pontiac. All together would fall upon the English, taking care not to harm the French who lived in the fort. The Hurons and the Potawatomies were to divide into two bands— one to go down the river to cut off those who should come from that way, the other to remain around the fort at a distance to kill those who were working outside. In all the villages, the war song was to be chanted.

After plans were made, each nation withdrew to its village, re-solved to carry out the orders of the great chief. But whatever pre-cautions they took against being discovered, God brought it about that they were discovered. An Ottawa Indian named Mahiganne, who was displeased at the evil behavior of his tribe, came Friday night—unbeknown to the other Indians—to the gate of the fort, and he asked to speak to the commander. The gate was opened and he was conducted to Mr. Gladwin, the commander-in-chief. He then explained the conspiracy of the Indians, and how they had sworn the destruction of the English. The commander thanked him and wanted to reward him with gifts. The Indian would not take any, and begged the commander not to betray him.

The commander, after he had heard this report, which seemed to be true, gave orders at once that the guard should be doubled at daybreak, that there should be two sentries at each big gate, and that the two small gates should be closed. This was quickly done. The officers were told to inspect the arms of their troops and warn them to be ready to appear at the first roll of the drum. All of this was to be done without any commotion so the Indians coming into the fort might not notice that their plans were discovered. The orders were carried out so well that the French did not know anything about it.

May 7.

The fatal day arrived for the English and perhaps for the French. Pontiac, who believed his designs still a secret, ordered in the morning that all his men should chant the war song, paint themselves, and put feathers in their hair.

169

Toward ten o'clock in the morning he came in his trappings to the fort to ask for a council, and it was granted. He and his men entered a house where Mr. Gladwin, commander-in-chief, waited with some of his officers. All were aware of the bold designs of Pontiac and had arms concealed in their pockets. The rest of the officers were busy readying their troops.

Once in council, Pontiac—thinking that it was about time for all of his people to have taken positions for the attack—went out to see for himself, and to give the signal to attack. He then saw some commotion toward the drill-ground and wondered what it might be. He saw that the troops were under arms and drilling. This maneuver showed him that he was surely discovered, and his project defeated. He was forced to re-enter the council room, where his men were waiting only for the cry to attack. They were greatly surprised when they saw him come back. Without saying good bye, they walked out of the gate to regain their village.

Pontiac, upon his return to the village, was overwhelmed by rage. He looked like a lioness robbed of all her whelps.

> *Foiled in his plan to surprise the English garrison, Chief Pontiac and his warriors soon began a siege of the fort at Detroit, which lasted for five months. The English managed to hold the isolated outpost at Detroit, but a number of other English forts soon fell before a widespread Indian onslaught.*

ATTACK ON MACKINAC

Alexander Henry   1763

Chief Pontiac succeeded in mustering Ottawas, Pota-
watomies, Hurons and Chippewas into a broad con-
federacy of Indian nations that also included Senecas,
Miamis, Weas, Kickapoos, Shawnees, Delawares, Kas-
kaskias, Cahokias, Peorias, Muncees and Missisaugis.
These tribes planned surprise attacks against more than
a dozen English forts between Lake Michigan and cen-
tral Pennsylvania. At the time, the young Alexander
Henry was trading with Indians at the fort at Mack-
inac.

Soon after my arrival at Mackinac, a Chippewa chief
named Wawatam had come to my house, betray-
ing signs of strong personal regard. His visits continued for some time, and then one day he brought his whole family,
with a large gift of furs, maple sugar and dried meat. Laying these
in a heap, he made a speech, telling me that some years before, while
fasting in solitude, he had dreamed of adopting an Englishman as
his son, brother and friend. He said from the moment he first saw
me, he recognized me as the person whom the Great Spirit had
pointed out to be his brother. He said he hoped I would not refuse
his gift, and that I would become one of his family.

I declared my willingness to have so good a man for my friend
and brother, and I made a gift in return. Wawatam then left me,

and soon after this visit, his family set out on their winter hunt. I did not see Wawatam again until June 2nd, 1763.

In the spring of 1763, traders arriving at Mackinac from different parts of the country brought word that the Indians were growing hostile to the English. One trader told Major Etherington of a plan, fully conceived, to destroy him, his garrison, and all the English in the Upper Country. The major, believing such reports to come from idle or ill-disposed persons, threatened to send the next person with such a report to Detroit as a prisoner. The English garrison at Mackinac at that time included 90 privates, two subalterns, and the major. There were also four English traders at the fort. As strong as we were, few of us worried about the Indians, who had only small arms.

Meanwhile, Indians from every quarter were arriving daily at Mackinac in unusual numbers. They appeared to be friendly as they visited the fort to trade their pelts. Yet on one occasion I took the liberty to tell Major Etherington that they should not be trusted, that no less than 400 Indians were camped around the fort. In reply he only ridiculed me for my timidity.

Yet I must admit that I too ignored the warning signs. I had almost forgotten my brother, Wawatam, when on the 2nd day of June he came again to my house. This time he was sad and thoughtful. He said he had just returned from his wintering ground. I asked about his health, but without answering, he said he was very sorry to find me at Mackinac. He asked me to leave the next morning with him and his family for Sault Ste. Marie. He also asked whether the major had heard any bad news. He said that during the winter, he himself had been disturbed often by the noise of evil birds. I did not pay enough attention to my visitor. The Indian manner of speech is so figurative that I did not understand his warning. I said I would not think of leaving for the Sault before my clerks arrived at Mackinac. I turned a deaf ear, leaving Wawatam to shed a few tears and depart alone.

The next day, Indians in great numbers entered the fort to buy small axes, and to see silver armbands and other valuable trade goods. Yet they bought none of the jewelry, saying they would call again the next day. That night I turned over in my mind the visit of Wawatam. I was uneasy, but none of it made me understand the serious business at hand.

The next day was the 4th of June, the king's birthday. The morning was sultry. A Chippewa came to tell me that his nation was going to play a game of la crosse with the Sauks for a high wager. He invited me to watch, adding that the major would be there and would bet on the side of the Chippewas. The match was to be played just outside the fort. I did not go, but instead I wrote letters, because a canoe was about to depart for Montreal. Many of the soldiers, however, went outside the fort to watch.

La crosse is an Indian game played with a ball and rackets. Each team has its post, and each tries to hurl the ball to the post of the opponent. The game is played with great violence and noise, and in the heat of the contest, the ball may be struck in any direction. Consequently, there was no alarm among the English when the ball was tossed over the stockade of the fort, and was followed instantly by the players, who ran in through the open gate, all eager, all struggling, all shouting.

Suddenly, the Indians pulled weapons from under the blankets of their women, turned, and began slaughtering the startled English soldiers.

From inside my house, I suddenly heard an Indian war cry, then a noise of general confusion. Going to my window, I saw a crowd of Indians inside the fort, furiously cutting down and scalping every Englishman they found. I had in my house a fowling piece, loaded with swan shot. I seized it and held it, waiting to hear the drum beat to arms. In this dreadful interval, I saw several of my countrymen fall, and more than one struggling between the knees of an Indian, as they were scalped while yet living.

Finally, losing hope of seeing any resistance made, and knowing that no effort of my own could help against 400 Indians, I thought only of hiding. Amid the slaughter that was raging, I noticed many of the French Canadians calmly looking on, neither opposing the Indians nor suffering injury. From this I decided to seek safety in one of their houses. One of the French, Monsieur Langlade, was my neighbor. I ran into his house, where I found his whole family at

173

Massacre at Michilimackinak, by Robert Thom

the windows, gazing at the scene of blood before them. I begged Langlade to hide me until the heat of the moment had passed. He looked at me for a moment, turned again to the window, shrugged his shoulders, and said he could do nothing for me.

This moment of despair was interrupted by a Pawnee woman, a slave of Langlade's, who beckoned me to follow her. She led me to a door and told me to hide myself in the attic, locking the door as she left. From this shelter I had a view of the fort, and I saw in terrible forms the ferocious triumphs of barbarian conquerors. The dead were scalped and mangled. The dying were writhing and shrieking under the knife and tomahawk. From the bodies of some, the butchers were drinking blood, scooped up in the hollow of joined hands and quaffed amid shouts of rage and victory. I was shaken with horror and with fear. I believed that I would soon experience the same suffering.

It was not long before all the English soldiers were killed, and there arose a cry of "All is finished." At that instant I heard some Indians enter the house. I could hear everything that happened below me. The Indians asked whether there was an Englishman in the house. Langlade replied that he did not know of any, but that they could look for themselves. He then brought them to the attic door. As he searched for the key, I quickly hid beneath a heap of birch-bark vessels used in making maple sugar. In another instant the door was opened, and four Indians walked in, all armed with tomahawks and all besmeared with blood. I could scarcely breath, yet I thought the sound of my throbbing heart would give me away. The Indians walked all around the attic, telling Langlade how many English soldiers they had killed and how many scalps they had taken. Finally they left, and I heard the door closed and locked a second time—a barrier between me and my fate.

I was exhausted by the suspense, so I threw myself on a feather bed on the floor and fell asleep. I slept till dusk, when I was awakened by a second opening of the door. The person who now entered was Langlade's wife. She was much surprised at finding me, but she told me not to worry. She said she hoped I might escape. I begged her to send me water, which she did.

175

As night advanced, a shower of rain began to fall. I lay on the bed, pondering my situation, but unable to think of a way to save my life. Fleeing to Detroit would not succeed: Detroit was 400 miles away, through the country of an enemy in arms, where the first man to meet me would kill me. Once again, fatigue of mind brought me further sleep, and suspended my cares.

As morning returned, I was again on the rack of anxiety. At sunrise I heard the family stirring, and soon after that I heard Indian voices, telling Langlade they had not found my hapless self among the dead. They supposed that I was hidden somewhere. As soon as the Indians mentioned me, Langlade's wife declared to her husband, in French, that he should deliver me up to them. She said if the Indians would think that he had hidden me, they might take revenge on her children, and it was better that I should die than they. Langlade agreed, and he told the Indians that I had come to his house without his knowledge. He said he would put me into their hands. He then began climbing the stairs, with the Indians following at his heels.

I now resigned myself to my fate, arose from the bed, and presented myself in full view. The Indians who entered were all drunk and entirely naked except about the waist. One of them, a man named Wenniway, was more than six feet tall, and had his entire face and body blackened with charcoal and grease, except for a pair of white spots encircling each eye. This man walked up to me and seized me with one hand by my collar, while in the other hand he held a large carving knife, as if to plunge it into my breast. His eyes were fixed steadfastly on mine. After some seconds of the most anxious suspense, he dropped his arm, saying, "I will not kill you." He added that he had fought in battles against the English, he had brought away many scalps, and he had lost a brother in the fighting. He said he would take me with him and he would name me after his dead brother.

A reprieve on any terms placed me among the living and gave me back the sustaining voice of hope. Wenniway then ordered me to his lodge, where the Indians were all mad with liquor. Death again threatened me. I begged Langlade to let me stay in his house, and both he and Wenniway agreed, so I climbed back up the attic stairs to be as far as possible from the drunken Indians.

I was there less than an hour when I was called below by an Indian, who said that Wenniway had sent him to fetch me, and that I must leave the fort with him. This Indian had owed me a debt, and a short time before I had scolded him for his lack of honesty. He had said then that he would "pay" me before long. His speech now came fresh to my mind. I told Langlade that I thought the fellow had a design against my life, but Langlade answered, "You are not your own master, and you must do as you are ordered." The Indian ordered me to undress myself, declaring that my coat and shirt would look better on him. I undressed and put on his clothes, rather than go out naked. (I soon learned that his motive for stripping me was to keep my clothes from being stained with my own blood.) I walked out, and he followed close behind, until we passed the gate of the fort. Then he seized me by the arm and pulled me violently away from the other Indians. After some 50 yards, I saw that we were approaching bushes and sand hills. I decided to go no further, but told the Indian that if he meant to murder me, he might as well strike me where I stood. He coolly replied that he would do just that. He pulled out a knife and held me in position for the intended blow. By some effort, too sudden and thoughtless to be remembered, I stopped his arm, gave him a sudden push, turned from him, and escaped from his grasp. I then ran toward the fort with all the swiftness in my power, with the Indian close at my heals. I expected every moment to feel his knife. I succeeded in entering the fort, where I saw Wenniway, and I ran to him for protection. Wenniway told my attacker to stop, but he continued to pursue me as we both ran circles around Wenniway. The enraged Indian made several strokes at me with his knife. The three of us drew near Langlade's house. The door was open, and I ran into it. There the Indian stopped his attack.

Again I lay down to sleep. Later that evening I was roused from my sleep and ordered down the stairs, where I was surprised to see Major Etherington, Mr. Bostwick and Lieutenant Leslie in the room below. They were among only 20 Englishmen who had been taken as prisoners. Seventy soldiers had been killed.

The next day the Chippewas offered us bread, but bread they had cut with the knives they had used in the massacre—knives still covered with blood. They moistened the blood with spittle, rubbed it on the bread, and told us to eat the blood of our countrymen. We were the sport and the victims of events that seemed more like dreams than realities.

On the 7th of June, an event occurred that gave me new hope. Toward noon, as the great Chippewa war chief was seated in Wenniway's lodge, my friend and brother, Wawatam, suddenly arrived. (In the days after the attack, I had often wondered what had become of him.) As Wawatam passed me, he gave me his hand, but then went immediately to sit by the great chief. They were silent as they smoked a pipe. Then Wawatam arose and left the lodge, saying to me, "Take courage."

An hour passed, and several more chiefs arrived. Wawatam then returned, followed by his wife, both loaded with merchandise which they laid in a heap before the chiefs. Wawatam gave the following speech:

"Friends and kinsmen: What shall I say? You know how I feel. You all have friends and brothers and children whom you love as yourselves. How would you feel if you saw your dearest friend, your brother, held as a slave, exposed every moment to insults and threats of death? See here is my friend and brother, among slaves, a slave himself!

"You all know that long before this war began, I adopted him as my brother. From that moment he became one of my family, so that nothing could break the cord which binds us. I am your relative, so he is your relative too. How can he be your slave?

"On the day when this war began, you were fearful that I would reveal the secret of your plans. You asked that I leave the fort and cross the lake. I agreed to do so, because you in command promised to protect my brother, to deliver him from all danger, and to give him safely to me.

178

"I now claim him. I come not with empty hands to ask for him. I bring these goods, to buy off every claim which any man may have on my brother as a prisoner."

Wawatam sat down, the pipes were filled and smoked, and silence followed. Then the war chief replied. "My brother: What you have spoken is true. I promised you that I would take care of your friend. We accept your present. You may take him home with you."

Wawatam thanked the chiefs, and taking me by the hand, he led me to his lodge.

FRIEND AND BROTHER

Alexander Henry   1763–64

Alexander Henry—isolated from his countrymen and surrounded by hostile Indians—was glad and grateful to be adopted into the family of the Wawatam, his Chippewa savior.

A few days after joining Wawatam's family, I was told that Indians were now arriving daily from Detroit. Some had lost relatives or friends in the war, and would certainly retaliate against any Englishman. I was advised to dress like an Indian, to escape future insult. I could not but consent to the proposal.

That very day Wawatam and his family made the change. My hair was cut off and my head was shaved, except for a spot on the crown. My face was painted with three or four colors, some of it red, some of it black. I was given a shirt, red with vermilion mixed with grease. A large necklace was put around my neck, and another hung on my breast. Both my arms were decorated with bands of silver, large ones above the elbows, smaller ones on the wrists. My legs were covered with leggings of scarlet cloth. Over all I wore a scarlet blanket, and on my head a large bunch of feathers. I regretted to part with my long hair, which I fancied to be ornamental, but the ladies of the village now thought my appearance improved and called me handsome, even among Indians.

Protected by this disguise, I returned to the fort to meet my French Canadian clerks, whom I expected to return with some of my property. I met them, but they brought me nothing. Nothing, I began to think, would be all that I would need for the rest of my life. To fish and to hunt, to collect a few skins and trade them for necessities—this was all I seemed destined to do.

I returned to the Indian village [on Mackinac Island] where food was scarce. We often went for 24 hours without eating. In the morning, when we had no food before us, the custom was to blacken our faces with charcoal, and to act as cheerful as though we had plenty. But hunger soon forced us to leave the island in search of food. At the Bay of Boutchitouay [St. Martin Bay] we found plenty of wildfowl and fish.

Wawatam's family included his wife, a daughter 13 years old, two sons (the eldest of whom had a wife) and myself. Wawatam alternately called me his brother, his son, and his friend.

While at the bay, Wawatam's daughter-in-law was taken in labor of her first child. The women quickly built a small lodge for her. The next morning we heard she was very ill, and the family became greatly alarmed for her, all the more so because cases of difficult labor are very rare among Indian women. During her distress, Wawatam asked me to go with him into the woods. On our way he told me that if he could find a snake, he could soon secure relief for his daughter-in-law. On reaching wet ground, we found a small garter snake. Wawatam seized it by the neck, and holding it fast as it coiled around his arm, he cut off its head and caught the blood in a cup. This done, he threw away the snake and carried home the blood, which he mixed with water. He gave one large spoonful to his daughter-in-law, then a second. Within an hour, a fine child was delivered. The next day, as we left the bay, the young mother helped load the canoe, barefoot, knee-deep in water, and in high spirits. Wawatam later told me that this remedy never failed.

The Indians are generally free from disorders. I never heard of one suffering from dropsy, gout or stone. Lung inflammations and rheumatism are their most common complaints, probably because they are so exposed to the cold and wet, sleeping on the ground and inhaling the night air.

Among all Indian nations, certain individuals claim to know the art of healing by sorcery. I once saw a performance in which the

181

Chippewa mother and baby, by George Catlin

Chippewa brave, by George Catlin

patient was a 12-year-old girl. After receiving a gift for his services, the sorcerer sat on the ground. Before him was placed a basin of water in which were three hollow bones, apparently from a swan's wing. In his hand was a rattle, with which he beat time to his medicine song. The sick child lay on a blanket, breathing hard, with a high fever. After singing for some time, the sorcerer took a bone, put one end to the breast of the girl and the other end to his mouth, and tried to suck the disorder from her. He suddenly seemed to force the bone into his mouth and swallow it. Upon its disappearance, he began to distort himself in the most frightful manner, to show his pain. With his rattle he struck his head, breast, sides and back, straining as if to vomit forth the bone. At last he pretended to throw up the bone. In the groove of the bone he found a small white object, like a piece of the quill of a feather. This was passed around, and the sorcerer gravely declared it to be the cause of the illness.

Whatever the faults of this sorcerer as an imposter, I must say that he earned his reward by dint of bodily labor. Unfortunately, the girl soon died.

Most Indians believe that the sorcerers, whom the French call *jongleurs* or jugglers, can inflict pain as well as remove it. They do so by drawing the figure of a person in sand or ashes, then pricking it with a sharp stick. The mischief once done, another sorcerer of equal pretensions can remove the pain by suction.

I must add that for flesh wounds the Indians effect astonishing cures. Much occurs that is fantastic, but the success of their practices indicates something that is real. At Sault Ste. Marie, I knew a man who in a quarrel suffered the stroke of an axe to his side. The axe was driven so deep that the wretch who held it could not pull it out, but left it in the wound and fled. Soon after, the victim was found and carried into the village. His eyes were fixed, his teeth were shut, and his case seemed desperate. A sorcerer immediately brought a medicine bag, and pulled from it a very white substance that he mixed with water. Forcing open the patient's mouth with a stick, he poured the mixture down his throat. In a short time, the wounded

184

man moved his eyes, and began to vomit, throwing up a small clump of clotted blood. The sorcerer then, and not before, examined the wound. I could see breath escaping from the wound, out of which hung a membrane. The sorcerer did not try to push this membrane back into place, but rather, he cut it away, minced it into small pieces, and made his patient swallow it. The man then was carried to his lodge, where I visited him daily. By the sixth day he could walk. Within a month he was quite well, although troubled with a cough.

I may add that the sorcerers themselves sometimes suffer from their practices. I saw one of them killed by a man who accused him of bringing death to his brother. In his rage, the accuser thrust his knife into the belly of the accused and ripped it open. The sorcerer caught his own bowels in his arms, and walked for some distance toward his lodge, gathering them up from time to time. He reached his lodge, and soon died within it.

In late August, with autumn at hand, Wawatam proposed going to his winter hunting ground, where our family would live alone. Our departure gave me the greatest joy, because I now could escape the frequent insults from the other Indians of the village.

We canoed along the east coast of Lake Michigan to the mouth of the River Aux Sables [Big Sable River], distant about 150 miles from Mackinac. On our voyage we passed several deep bays and rivers. The shores of the lake consist of mere sand, without plants, the sand drifting from one hill to another like snow in winter. The currents of the rivers that enter the lake are met and driven back by waves from the lake, while the sands of the shores are washed into the mouths of the rivers. Consequently, each river is able to force only a narrow passage into the lake, while it hollows out a basin behind the sand banks of one, two or three miles across. In those rivers we killed many wildfowl and beaver.

On entering the Big Sable River, Wawatam took a dog, tied its feet together, and threw it into the water, as he uttered a long prayer to the Great Spirit, asking his blessing on the hunt and his help in supporting the family through the dangers of the long winter. We camped 15 miles above the mouth of the river, where the principal

185

animals were elk, deer, bear, racoon, beaver and marten. As we hunted, I enjoyed a personal freedom I had not known before. I soon became as expert in Indian pursuits as the Indians themselves.

To kill the beaver we sometimes went up the river before nightfall. Then, when dusk came on, we let our canoe drift noiselessly down with the current. The beavers, abroad at that time of the evening, were not alarmed by the drifting canoe, and often passed within gun shot.

The most common way of taking the beaver is to break up its house, which has a dome-like roof that rises three to four feet above the water. This is done in winter, when the ice is strong enough to support hunters, and when beaver fur is in its prime. As the beaver house is being broken, the animals make their escape under water into one or more holes beneath the river bank. The holes are discovered by striking the ice along the bank, and where there are holes, a hollow sound is returned. The beavers must be pulled from the holes by hand, and the hunter is sometimes severely bitten.

The Indians say that the beaver is very jealous. If a strange male approaches a couple, a battle ensues, of which the female is an unconcerned spectator, not caring to which party the law of conquest may assign her. Among the beavers we killed, almost all the older males bore marks of violence. The Indians add that the male is as faithful as he is jealous, never mating with more than one female, while the female is always fond of strangers. The Indians say the beaver once could speak, but the Great Spirit took their speech away from them, so they would not grow wiser than men.

Racoon hunting was my own special duty. I usually went out before dawn with Wawatam's youngest son and the dogs. We seldom returned before sunset.

I gradually grew familiar with this kind of life, except for the lingering hope that I would some day be released from it. If I could have forgotten that I had once lived otherwise, I would have been as happy in this life as in any other.

On December 20th, we tallied the results of our hunt: 100 beaver skins, as many racoons, and a large amount of dried venison, all of which we placed on a scaffold to keep it from the wolves. We then decided to go on a hunting trip into the interior. Early the next morning bundles were made up by the women for each to carry. I noticed that my bundle was the lightest, and those carried by the women were the heaviest.

In three days we reached our camp, and while the women were busy erecting lodges, I took my gun and strolled away, telling Wawatam that I intended to look for fresh meat for supper. The sun was shining, so I had no fear of losing my way; but in following several tracks, expecting to find game at any instant, I wandered for quite a distance. It was not until sunset that I thought of returning. By then the sky had clouded over, and I was left without the sun for my guide. I started to walk as fast as I could, always expecting to see our camp, until at length it was so dark that I was running into trees.

I soon realized that I was lost, and I was alarmed by the thought that I was in a strange country, in danger of meeting hostile Indians. I made a fire with my flint, and laid down to sleep. That night it rained hard, and I lay awake, cold and wet. As soon as light appeared, I again started my journey, sometimes walking and sometimes running, bewildered, like a madman. Toward evening I reached the shore of a lake, but I had never heard of a lake in that part of the country, so I felt more lost than ever. I now decided to try to retrace my steps, so I turned my face directly away from the lake and held that direction as best I could.

Night came on and a heavy snow began to fall. I stopped to make a fire, and stripping a sheet of bark off a tree, I lay under it to shelter me from the snow. All night long wolves howled around me. They seemed to understand my misfortune. Amid thoughts most distracted, I finally fell asleep.

Yet it was not long before I awoke, refreshed, and wondering at the terror to which I had yielded. It seemed almost incredible, like a dream, that I could have failed to find my way. If I had not lost my senses, I would never have suffered for so long. I would have remembered the lessons of my Indian friend. He had taught me that the tops of pine trees generally lean toward the rising of the sun, that moss grows on the north sides of trees, and that the branches

187

of trees are most numerous and largest toward the south. I decided to direct my feet westward by these marks, convinced that I sooner or later would reach Lake Michigan.

I began my march at break of day. The snow lay a foot and a half deep. I trained my eyes on the trees. When their tops leaned different ways, I looked to the moss or to the branches, and by connecting one with another, I traveled with some confidence. That afternoon, to my inexpressible joy, the sun broke from behind the clouds. I had no more need to examine the trees.

In walking down the side of a high hill, I saw a herd of elk approaching. I hid in bushes, and as a large elk came near, I raised my gun. It misfired, because the priming was wet. The elk were not alarmed, so I reloaded, followed them, and aimed a second time. But now a disaster of the worst kind befell me. On attempting to fire, I found that I had lost the cock. Of all my sufferings, this seemed the most severe. I was in a strange country, I had not eaten for three days, and I did not know how far I would have to go for help. Now I could neither obtain food nor make a fire. Despair almost over-powered me, but soon I resigned myself into the hands of God, whose arm had so often saved me. I resumed my journey, wet, cold and hungry.

The sun was setting fast as I descended a hill, at the bottom of which was a small lake, entirely frozen over. On drawing near, I saw a beaver lodge in the middle of the lake, offering some faint prospect of food, but I soon found that it was already broken up. While I stood looking at it, I suddenly realized that I had seen it before. Turning my eyes around the place, I discovered a small tree, which I myself had cut down the autumn before, when I and my friends had taken the beaver.

I was no longer lost. Now I knew both the distance and the route to our camp. I only had to follow the course of a small stream that flowed from the camp to this lake on which I stood. An hour before, I had thought myself the most miserable of men. Now I wept for joy, and called myself the happiest.

That whole night and all the next day, I walked up the stream. At sunset I reached the camp. I was greeted with the warmest expressions of pleasure by the family, who had given me up for lost, after a long search for me.

After some days of rest I resumed the hunt, secure because snow had fallen, and I could always return by the way I went.

One day in January I noticed that the trunk of a very large pine tree had been torn by the claws of a bear. Looking closer, I saw a large opening in the upper part of the trunk. As there were no tracks in the snow, I concluded that a bear lay concealed in the tree. I returned to the lodge and reported my discovery. It was agreed that all the family would help in cutting down the tree, the girth of which was at least 18 feet. At first the women opposed the idea, because our axes weighed only a pound and a half. But the hope of finding a large bear and securing much needed oil from its fat, convinced them of the plan.

The next morning we surrounded the tree, both men and women, as many at a time as could chop at it. There we toiled like beavers, till the sun went down. The day's work carried us about half way through the trunk, and the next morning we renewed the attack. About two o'clock that afternoon the tree fell. For a few minutes, everything was quiet. I feared we would be disappointed, but as I walked toward the opening, a bear of extraordinary size came out. Before she had gone many yards, I shot her.

Once the bear was dead, all my assistants approached her. They took her head in their hands, stroking and kissing it several times, begging a thousand pardons for taking away her life, calling her their grandmother, and asking her not to blame them, since it was truly an Englishman who had put her to death. This ceremony did not last long, and if it was I who killed their grandmother, they themselves were not far behind in what remained to be done. The animal was skinned, and we found the fat six inches deep in several places. This fat loaded two of us, and the flesh was as much as four could carry.

As soon as we reached the lodge, the bear's head was adorned with all the family's trinkets, such as silver arm bands and belts of beads. Then it was put upon a scaffold within the lodge, for its reception.

189

The next morning no sooner appeared than preparations were made for a feast to the spirit of the dead bear. The lodge was cleaned and swept. A new wool blanket was spread under the head of the bear. The pipes were lit, and Wawatam blew tobacco smoke into the nostrils of the bear, telling me to do the same, thus to appease the anger of the bear. It was I, after all, who had killed her. I tried to convince my friend that the bear no longer had any life, and I assured him that I did not fear her anger. He, however, did not credit my first statement, and was not satisfied with my second.

At length, Wawatam began a speech, like an address to the spirits of his own dead relatives, but with one difference. Here he deplored the necessity under which men labor to destroy their friends, the animals. He added that this misfortune was unavoidable, since without it, men could not survive.

The speech ended, we all ate heartily of the bear's flesh. Even the head, after three days on the scaffold, was put into the kettle. The fat of the bear was melted down, and the oil filled six porcupine skins. Part of the meat was cut into strips and fire-dried, after which it was put into the oil, where it remained perfectly preserved for months.

The Chippewas call February the Moon of the Crusted Snow. In that month the snow can bear a man and dogs in pursuit of prey, and the stag is easily hunted, as his hooves break through at every step, and the sharp crust of the snow cuts his legs to the very bone. We sometimes killed 12 stags within two hours. By this means we soon had 4,000 weight of dried venison, to be carried on our backs along with the rest of our wealth for 70 miles, back to the shore of Lake Michigan.

Our venison and furs were to be traded at Mackinac, and it was now the season for carrying them to market. The women prepared our loads, and we began to carry them toward the lake, in stages. As we neared the lake, we stopped to make maple sugar. The women managed this process, as the men cut wood for fires, and hunted and fished. We were joined there by several lodges of Indians who had wintered nearby.

190

Soon afterward, an accident occurred which filled all the village with grief. A little child fell into a vat of boiling syrup. She was snatched out instantly, but with little hope for her recovery. So long as she lived, a continual feast was observed, made to the Great Spirit that he might save and heal the child. I was a constant guest at this feast, where I had trouble eating the great amount of food which, on such occasions, is put upon each man's dish. (The Indians are accustomed both to eating much, and to fasting much.) Sacrifices were offered to the Great Spirit. Dogs were killed and hung from the tops of poles, along with wool blankets and other objects.

The child soon died.

To keep the body from the wolves, it was placed on a scaffold, and it remained there until we went to Lake Michigan, on the shore of which was the family burial ground. A large grave was dug and lined with birch bark. The body of the child was laid on the bark, along with an axe, a pair of snow shoes, a small kettle filled with meat, several pairs of shoes, her own strings of beads, a carrying belt and a paddle. All was covered with bark. Two feet closer to the surface, logs were laid across, and these again were covered with bark, so the earth could not fall upon the corpse.

The last act before burial was performed by the mother. As she cried over the dead body of her child, she took from it a lock of hair. I tried to console her with the usual arguments: that the child was happy in being released from the miseries of this life, and that the child some day would be restored to her in another world, happy and everlasting. The mother answered that she knew it, and that with this lock of hair she would discover her daughter. She alluded to the day when some pious hand would place in her own grave this lock of hair, a small relic hallowed by a mother's tears.

While we remained on the border of the lake, a close watch was kept every night, in fear of a sudden attack by the English, who were expected to avenge the massacre at Mackinac. The old women had dreamed of such an attack. Amid these alarms, we learned of a real, though less dreaded enemy, discovered near our camp. It was a lynx, an animal which sometimes attacks and carries away Indian children. We immediately set off into the woods, about 20 in number. We

191

had gone less than a mile when the dogs found the lynx in a tree, and he was shot.

On April 25th we embarked for Mackinac. At Le Grande Traverse we met a large party of Indians, who were also alarmed, and who dared go no further for fear that they would be destroyed by the English. I was continually asked whether I knew of any plan to attack them. They believed that I knew the future, and that in dreams I learned of far-away events. They were suspicious when I pled ignorance, so at last I told them that there was no enemy nearby. Thus encouraged, they embarked for Mackinac.

Some days later, when I was at Sault Ste. Marie, a canoe arrived from Niagara. Everyone was anxious to hear the news, so the strangers in the canoe were summoned to council. They arrived, and after a long silence, one of them picked up a belt of wampum beads and spoke thus: "My friends and brothers. I come with this belt, from our great English father, Sir William Johnson. He asked me to come to you as his ambassador, to tell you that he is making a great feast at Fort Niagara; that his kettles are ready and his fires are lit. He invites you to the feast along with your friends. He advises you to seize this opportunity. Otherwise he will not fail to destroy you, for the English are on the march with a great army. Before the fall of the leaf, they will be at Mackinac, and the Iroquois will be with them."

This speech greatly alarmed the Indians of the Sault. Many argued that little time should be lost in sending ambassadors to Fort Niagara. But the decision was so important that it called for more than human knowledge. Accordingly, the Indians prepared to solemnly invoke the spirit of the Great Turtle. The first thing done was to build a large wigwam, within which was placed a kind of tent for use by the sorcerer. The tent was made of moose skins hung over five poles, each from a different kind of tree; each was ten feet tall and planted two feet in the ground.

With the approach of night, the ceremony began. Fires were kindled around the tent to give light within. Almost the whole village assembled within the wigwam, myself among the rest. Soon the sorcerer appeared, almost naked, and he crept under the tent skins on his hand and knees. His head was scarcely inside when the tent, massive as it was, began to shake. The skins were no sooner let down than the sounds of many voices were heard beneath them, some yelling, some barking like dogs, some howling like wolves. Mingled in this horrible concert were screams and sobs of despair, anguish and the sharpest pain. Words, too, were uttered, as if from human lips, but in a strange tongue. At some voices, all the Indians hissed, recognizing them to belong to evil and lying spirits which deceive mankind.

After some time, the confused and frightful noises were followed by perfect silence. Then a voice, not heard before, seemed to manifest the arrival of a new character in the tent. It was a low and feeble voice, like the cry of a young puppy. The sound was no sooner heard than the Indians all clapped their hands for joy, exclaiming that this was the Chief Spirit, the Turtle, the spirit that never lies!

The questions were to come from the chief of the village, who was silent until after he placed tobacco inside the tent, as a sacrifice to the spirit. He then told the sorcerer to ask whether or not the English were preparing to make war upon the Indians, and whether or not there were many English troops at Fort Niagara.

These questions were posed by the sorcerer, and the tent instantly shook. For some seconds it rocked so violently that I expected to see it leveled. I supposed that all this would be a prelude to the answers, but a terrific cry soon announced the departure of the Great Turtle. A quarter of an hour elapsed in silence, and I waited impatiently for the next scene in this deception. When the spirit returned, its voice was again heard, making a long speech in a strange tongue, interpreted by the sorcerer. The sorcerer informed us that the spirit, during his short absence, had crossed Lake Huron and proceeded as far as Fort Niagara, at the head of Lake Ontario, and from there to Montreal. At Fort Niagara he had seen no great number of soldiers, but on descending the St. Lawrence River to Montreal, he had found the river covered with boats, and the boats filled with soldiers in numbers like the leaves of the trees. They were on their way up the river, to make war on the Indians.

193

The chief posed a third question: "If Indians visit Sir William Johnson, will they be received as friends?"

The spirit, without a fresh journey to Fort Niagara, was able in an instant to give the most favorable answer: "Sir William Johnson will fill their canoes with presents: with blankets, kettles, guns, gun powder, shot, and large barrels of rum, such that the strongest of Indians will not be able to lift. Every man will return safely to his family."

At this the joy was universal. Amid the clapping of hands, a hundred voices exclaimed, "I will go too! I will go too!"

Questions of public interest resolved, individuals were permitted to ask about absent friends, or the fate of those who were sick. (I noticed that the answers allowed much latitude of interpretation.) Amid the general curiosity, I yielded to my own anxiety for the future. After making my offering of tobacco, I asked if I would ever revisit my native country. The tent shook as usual, after which I received this answer: "Take courage, and fear no danger, for nothing will happen to hurt you. In the end, you will reach your friends and country in safety." These assurances wrought so strongly on my gratitude, that I made an extra offering of tobacco.

The Great Turtle continued to be consulted until near midnight, when all the crowd dispersed to their lodges.

It was decided that on the 10th of June, 1764, I was to embark for Fort Niagara with 16 Indian envoys. My departure fixed upon, I packed up my wardrobe consisting of two shirts, a pair of leggings and a blanket. I took a gun and ammunition, and I gave what I did not need to my host, Wawatam. I also returned the silver arm bands, with which the family had decorated me.

The family congratulated me on this opportunity to escape. My brother lit his pipe and presented it to me, saying, "My brother, this may be the last time that ever you and I smoke from the same pipe. I am sorry to part with you. You know the affection I hold for you. You know the dangers that I and my family have risked for you, to save you from your enemies. I am happy that my efforts have not been in vain."

194

We exchanged farewells; I with the most grateful sense of the many acts of goodness they had shown me. All the family went with me to the beach. The canoes no sooner put off than Wawatam began a prayer to the Great Spirit. He beseeched the Great Spirit to care for me, his brother, until we should meet again. He continued his prayer—even after I could no longer hear him.

195

UNKNOWN
DOMINION

Jonathan Carver   1766–67

At age 57, a New Englander named Jonathan Carver set out to explore the Upper Country for Great Britain.

No sooner was the war with France concluded than I began to consider how I might continue my service, and help Great Britain take advantage of its vast acquisition of territory. I decided, as proof of my zeal, to explore the most unknown parts of the dominion.

I began my travels from Michillimackinac [Mackinac], a fort located between Lake Huron and Lake Michigan. Michillimackinac in the Chippewa language means "great turtle." The place receives its name from an island resembling a turtle, which is within sight of the fort.

I left this fort on September 3rd, in company with traders bound for Fort La Bay, at the south end of a bay that the English call Green Bay. It is so named for its appearance, for on leaving Mackinac in the spring season when the trees have not yet budded, you arrive at Green Bay 14 days later to find the country covered with the finest greenery.

At the entrance to Green Bay from the lake is a string of islands about 30 miles in length, called the Grand Traverse. These islands aid the passage of canoes by sheltering them from violent winds. On the largest and best of these islands [Washington Island] stands a village of the Ottawas, where I was met with a strange reception. As our canoes approached the shore, the Indians began to fire their muskets, running from one tree to another, shouting and behaving as though in the heat of battle. The balls flew but a few yards above our heads. I was greatly surprised, and about to order their fire returned, when a trader told me this was their customary way to greet chiefs from other nations. When I considered it in this light, I was pleased with the respect paid me.

An Ottawa chief received me with every courtesy he could possibly show a stranger. I gave his people spiritous liquors, and they made merry, and danced the greatest part of the night. In the morning the chief went with me to the shore, and as I embarked he offered up a solemn and fervent prayer on my behalf. He prayed that the Great Spirit would favor me with a prosperous voyage; that he would give me a clear sky and smooth waters by day; that by night I would lie down on a beaver blanket and enjoy pleasant dreams; and that I would find protection under the great pipe of peace.

I must say that although Europeans have horrid ideas of the ferocity of these so-called savages, I received from every tribe of them the most courteous hospitality. I am convinced that they are friendly toward strangers, until they are contaminated by the example and the liquor of their more refined neighbors. I do recognize their cruelty to their enemies, a failure that is too deeply rooted in their minds ever to be removed.

The Ottawas make the best bread I have ever tasted. While their corn is in the milk, they slice off the kernels, knead them into paste, shape the paste into cakes, wrap the cakes in basswood leaves, and put them in hot embers, where they are soon baked.

We followed the southeast coast of Green Bay, where the land is covered with a heavy growth of hemlock, pine, spruce and fir. The land at the bottom of this bay is very fertile, the country level, the view extensive and pleasing. Sumac grows here in great plenty. The natives gather its leaf when it turns red, and mix it with their tobacco. They also scrape bark from a kind of red willow, which the French call "bois rouge," and they mix it with tobacco for their winter smoking.

197

Winnebago camp, by Seth Eastman

On September 20th I left Green Bay and proceeded up the Fox River, still in company with traders and Indians. The river between Green Bay and Lake Winnebago is full of rocks and very rapid. Near its banks the land is very good, thinly wooded with hickory, oak and hazel.

On the 25th I arrived at the great village of the Winnebagoes, located on a small island at the east end of Lake Winnebago, [the site of Menasha, Wisconsin]. A queen rules this tribe. She received me with great civility. She was a small, ancient woman. The day after my arrival I held a council with the chiefs, at which the queen asked only a few questions. Women are not allowed to sit in councils except when invested with supreme authority, and then they do not make speeches.

I stayed four days with the Winnebagoes, learning about their origin, language and customs. I concluded that they once lived in a province of New Mexico, and were driven northward more than a century ago. The Winnebagoes are closely allied with the Sioux, even though they now live 600 miles distant. Their language differs from that of every other Indian nation. It is a very uncouth, guttural jargon, which none of their neighbors will attempt to learn. The Winnebagoes hate the Spaniards. They told me they have made many raids to the southwest. An old chief said that 46 winters ago, he and 50 warriors marched toward the southwest for three moons. As they were crossing a plain, they saw men on horseback who were of the Black People—for so they call the Spaniards. The Winnebagoes hid until night, then rushed upon the Spaniards, killed most of them, and took 80 horses loaded with what they called "white stone." This I think was silver, for the chief said the bridles on the Spaniards' horses were ornamented with this same stone. Once the Winnebagoes were out of reach of the Spaniards who had escaped their fury, they left behind the useless burden of white stone in a woods, mounted the horses, and returned to their own country. I concluded that the party they defeated was the Spanish caravan that each year carries to Mexico the silver which the Spaniards find in great quantities on the mountains near the headwaters of the Colorado River.

We left the Winnebago village on September 29th and proceeded up the Fox River. Above Lake Winnebago the river is so serpentine that our canoes sometimes had to travel five miles to advance just a quarter of a mile. In some places the canoes could hardly pass through the stalks of wild rice, growing here in great abundance, very tall and thick. This river is the greatest resort for wild fowl that I saw in all my travels. Frequently the sun would be darkened by them for minutes at a time. The country around is very fertile, and in no part very wooded, yet it could supply enough wood for any number of settlers. Deer and bear are very numerous, and a great many beaver are taken.

An Indian told me that 80 years ago this country was the home of the united bands of Outagamies [Foxes] and Saukies [Sauks]. French missionaries and traders had suffered many insults from those people, so a party of French and Indians marched to avenge their wrongs. They set off from Green Bay in the winter, marching 50 miles over the snow. They surprised the Foxes and Sauks, and killed or captured most of them. As they returned with captives, an Indian chief allied with the French stopped to drink at a brook, as his companions went on. A captive Fox woman saw this and suddenly seized the chief by an exquisitely susceptible part, as he stooped to drink. The chief, in extreme torture, could not call out to his friends. She held him fast, until he died on the spot. Then she cut the bonds of her fellow prisoners, and they made their escape. This heroine was ever after treated by her nation as its deliverer, and she was made a chieftess in her own right.

The carrying place between the Fox River and the Ouisconsin [Wisconsin] River is not more than a mile and three quarters [at the site of Portage, Wisconsin]. On the 8th of October we put our canoes into the Wisconsin River, which flows with a smooth but strong current. The water is very clear, and through it you can see a fine and sandy bottom, free of rocks. In the river are a few islands, quite wooded. The land near the river seems to be excellent, but at a distance it is full of mountains, said to abound in lead.

The next day we arrived at the great village of the Sauks [near the site of Prairie du Sac, Wisconsin]. This is the largest and best built Indian village I ever saw. It contains 90 lodges, each large enough for several families, each built of hewn planks neatly joined and covered compactly with bark to keep out the most penetrating rain. Just outside the doors are comfortable platforms where the Indians sit and smoke their pipes. The streets are regular and wide, more like a civilized town than the abode of savages. In their fields, neatly laid out next to their lodges, they grow great quantities of corn, beans and melons. This village is the best market for traders to buy food within 800 miles.

Every summer the Sauks raise 300 warriors, and invade the territories of the Illinois and Pawnee nations, returning with many slaves. Yet those peoples often retaliate, and in their turn destroy many Sauks. This, I think, is the reason why the Sauk tribe grows no faster.

While I stayed here, I saw some mountains that lie about 15 miles to the south [Blue Mounds]. I climbed one of the highest of these, and had an extensive view of the country. For many miles nothing could be seen but smaller mountains, free of trees, that appeared from a distance like hay stacks. Only a few groves of hickory and stunted oak covered some of the valleys. Lead is so plentiful here that I saw it lying on the streets in the Sauk village.

On October 10th we proceeded down river, and the next day we reached a village of the Foxes [near the site of Wauzeka, Wisconsin]. This village contained 50 lodges, but most were deserted. Lately an epidemic had raged among these people, and carried off more than half. Most of the survivors had retired into the woods to avoid the contagion.

On the 15th we entered that vast river, the Mississippi. On its east bank, near the mouth of the Wisconsin, is a place the French call La Prairie du Chien, or Plain of the Dog. Here is a large village of Foxes, containing about 300 families, where I saw many horses of good size and shape. This town is the great market where many tribes, even those from the most remote branches of the Mississippi, gather annually at the end of May to sell their furs to the traders. They do not always make their sales here. At a general council the chiefs decide whether it is more in their interest to sell the furs at Prairie du Chien, or to carry them on to Louisiana or to Mackinac.

201

Minnesota River, by Seth Eastman

All Indians who happen to meet at Prairie du Chien, even those at war with each other, are obliged to restrain their hatred and forego violence. This long-standing rule is for their mutual benefit, because without it no trade could take place.

At Prairie du Chien I left the traders, bought a canoe, and proceeded up the Mississippi River with two servants. Mountains range on both sides of the Mississippi. In some places they are near the river, and in others they lie at a distance. The bluffs in many places resemble old, ruined towers. One side of a mountain may be an amazing precipice, while the opposite side is covered with the finest grass and a few groves of trees, near which herds of deer and elk are seen feeding. From the top of a mountain one can see the most beautiful and expansive view imaginable: verdant plains, fruitful meadows, numerous islands all abounding with trees that yield great quantities of fruit—nut trees, the maple which produces sugar, vines loaded with rich grapes, and plum trees bending under their burdens. Most beautiful of all is this fine river, flowing gently below, reaching as far as the eye can see, attracting your admiration and exciting your wonder.

On the first of November I arrived at Lake Pepin, a wide part of the Mississippi River. Great numbers of water fowl are seen on this lake and on the adjacent rivers: cranes, swans, geese, brants and ducks. In nearby groves are many turkeys and partridges. On the plains are the largest buffaloes of any in America.

Near the mouth of the River St. Croix live three bands of the Nadowessie [Sioux] Indians, called the River Bands: the Nehogata-wonahs, the Mawtawbauntowahs and the Shahsweentowahs. I stayed with the Mawtawbauntowahs for a day or two. During this stay, their scouts suddenly returned and warned that a large party of Chippewa warriors—"enough to swallow us all up"—was close at their heels and about to attack their little camp. The chiefs asked me to lead them into battle. In this dilemma I chose the middle course: I asked the Sioux to let me go meet with the Chippewas and try to avert their fury. To this they reluctantly agreed, convinced that my efforts would be in vain. Taking my French servant with me, I hurried toward the Chippewas, and approached them with the pipe of peace.

203

They lay scattered about, and I could see they were very numerous, and many were armed with muskets. Eight or ten chiefs came toward me in a friendly manner. We held a long conversation, and I succeeded in some measure to mollify their hatred. They agreed to turn back without accomplishing their savage purposes. Happily successful, I returned to the Sioux, but I suggested that they instantly move their camp to some other part of the country, in case their enemies should break the promise they had given. The Sioux immediately started to strike their tents. When I had seen them on board their canoes, I pursued my route.

Not far from the mouth of the St. Croix is the burying ground of several bands of Sioux. These people have no fixed home. They live in tents and stay just a few months in any one spot. Yet they always bring the bones of their dead to this place. They bury their dead in the spring, when the chiefs meet here to settle affairs for the following summer.

Twenty miles above the mouth of the River St. Croix is the River St. Pierre, called by the natives Waddapawmenesotor [Minnesota River]. It falls into the Mississippi from the west. This is a fair, large river that flows through the country of the Sioux, a most delightful country. Wild rice grows here in abundance. At a little distance from the river are hills from which you have beautiful views. Near a branch of this river, called Marble River [in what is now Pipestone County, Minnesota], is a mountain from which the Indians get a sort of red stone, out of which they hew the bowls of their pipes. This country also abounds in a blue clay that serves the Indians for paint. Blue is regarded as a mark of peace, as it resembles the blue of the sky, a symbol of peace.

Near the mouth of the Minnesota River I overtook a young Winnebago chief who was traveling as ambassador to the Sioux. He agreed to go with me to see the Falls of St. Anthony, because his curiosity had been excited by accounts of this waterfall. We were forced to leave our canoes because of the ice on the river, so we went by land to this wonderful place [at the site of Minneapolis].

Fifteen miles before we reached the falls, we could hear the noise of the water. I was greatly surprised when I approached this astonishing work of nature, but I had little time to indulge my emotions, as my attention was drawn to the behavior of my companion. The young chief began a prayer to the Great Spirit, whose home he imagined this falls to be. He said he had come a long way to adore the Great Spirit, and now he would make the best offerings in his power. He first threw his pipe into the river, then his roll of tobacco, his bracelets, a necklace of beads, and last, his earrings. In short, he offered to his god every part of his dress that was valuable. During this offering he smote his chest with great violence, and threw his arms all about. He continued his adorations, and finally concluded them with fervent petitions that the Great Spirit protect us on our travels, give us a bright sun, a blue sky and calm waters. We then smoked my pipe in honor of the Great Spirit. I doubt not that the young chief's offerings and prayers were as acceptable to the universal God of mankind, as if they had been made with greater pomp, or in a consecrated place.

This beautiful cataract is 250 yards across. Its waters fall 30 feet, and the rapids below add to the descent. A little distance below the falls is a small island with many oak trees—every branch full of eagle nests. Here the eagles are safe from the attacks of man or beast, guarded by the rapids which the Indians never attempt to pass. The eagles find a constant supply of food in the animals and fish that are dashed to pieces by the falls.

The country around the falls is extremely beautiful, composed of gentle hills and groves of trees. I wished that I could enjoy this glorious sight in a better season, while the trees and hillocks were clad in nature's gayest dress. Yet even in November, the enchanting spot exceeded my warmest expectations.

I then proceeded northward on foot for 60 miles, seeing many deer and caribou, and some elk. The country abounds in beaver, otter and other furs. I soon learned that the goods I had been promised from Mackinac had not arrived, so I was forced to give up all thought of proceeding farther to the northwest. Instead, I descended the Mississippi and spent much of the winter with a band of Sioux at the Minnesota River. The next spring I canoed to Prairie du Chien for supplies, then returned to the mouth of the Chippewa River,

205

where I engaged an Indian guide and ordered him to steer toward the Ottawa Lakes, which lie near the head of this river. The country along the Chippewa River is very level, and on its banks lie fine meadows with the largest herds of buffalo and elk I ever saw. This country is called the "Road of War" between the Chippewa and the Sioux, who are continually at war with each other.

In July I crossed a number of small lakes and carrying places, and came to a head branch of the River St. Croix. I descended this branch to a fork, then ascended another branch to its source. On both these rivers I discovered deposits of virgin copper.

I then came to a small brook, which my guide thought might lead us to Lake Superior. At first the water was so scanty that my canoe would not float in it, but by stopping up several old beaver dams I was able to proceed. In a short time the water increased to a most rapid river [Bois Brule River] which we descended to Lake Superior.

The country from the Ottawa Lakes to Lake Superior is very uneven and thickly covered with woods. All the wilderness between the Mississippi River and Lake Superior is called by the Indians the Mosquito Country, and I thought it most justly named. I never saw or felt so many of those insects in my life.

I then coasted around the West Bay of Lake Superior. At the end of July I arrived at the Grand Portage on the northwest shore of Lake Superior, so named because those who go on the northwest trade carry their canoes and baggage about nine miles there to reach some small lakes. These waters eventually descend into Hudson's Bay. At Grand Portage I was again disappointed, for I was unable to buy any goods from traders arriving from Mackinac. I was again forced to give up my plans, and so I returned to Mackinac.

Lake Superior is said to be the largest body of fresh water on the globe. The water in general appears to lie on a bed of rocks. When the weather was calm and the sun shone bright, I could sit in my canoe and plainly see huge piles of stones beneath six fathoms of water. My canoe seemed to be suspended in air. As I looked through this limpid medium, my head swam and my eyes could no longer behold the dazzling scene.

206

There are many islands on this lake. The Indians have never settled on them, or even landed on them to hunt. They suppose these islands to be the home of the Great Spirit, and they tell many ridiculous stories of enchantment and magic experienced by Indians who were forced to take shelter from storms on them. This lake is as affected by storms as the Atlantic Ocean. The waves run as high, and are as dangerous to ships.

In September I canoed along the north and east coast of Lake Superior, and I arrived at the Falls of St. Marie [Sault Ste. Marie] in the beginning of October. From here I leisurely paddled back to Mackinac, and arrived there at the beginning of November, 1767, having been 14 months on this tour, having travelled almost 4,000 miles, and visited 12 Indian nations.

FUR
TRADER

Peter Pond   1773–75

*Six years after Jonathan Carver's expedition through
the Upper Country, the same route was followed and
described by Peter Pond. Pond's purpose was business
rather than exploration, for Pond was a fur trader.*

W e coasted along the north side of Lake Huron until we arrived at Mackinac, where I
found my trade goods had arrived safely
from New York. Here I saw many hundred people of all kinds. Some
were trading with tribes that had come great distances to market
their furs, skins, maple sugar, dried venison and bear's grease. Others
were equipping canoes to send to different parts of the country, there
to pass the winter with the Indians. I divided my goods and fitted
out 12 large canoes for different parts of the Mississippi River. Each
canoe was made of birch bark with white cedar ribs. Each could
carry 7,000 pounds.

In September I had my small fleet ready to cross Lake Michigan
to Green Bay, having employed nine clerks for different parts of the
north and west country. In three or four days we arrived at the mouth
of the bay, near a small French village.

After two days we ascended the Fox River until we came to a
village of people called Puans [Winnebagoes] at the east end of a
lake by the same name [Lake Winnebago]. These people are unique

208

among their neighbors. They speak a hard, uncouth language scarcely to be learned by any other people. I asked the oldest Frenchmen about the natural history of these people, and I was told they once lived west of the Missouri River. There they had eternal disputes with their neighbors, and at last had to flee to this lake where they now live.

Once when Captain George Turnbull commanded at Mackinac, a small band of Winnebagoes arrived there. The captain couldn't find an interpreter who understood them, and at length he said he had a mind to send for an old Highland Scot soldier who spoke little but his own harsh tongue. The captain said perhaps the Scot might understand the Winnebagoes, for their languages sounded much the same.

We ascended the Fox River until we came to a piece of high ground where the Winnebagoes bury their dead [now Butte des Morts, Winnebago County, Wisconsin]. We stopped awhile, and found some of that nation there to pay respects to a departed friend. They filled their pipe and began their ceremony by pointing the stem upward, then toward the head of the grave, then east and west, north and south, after which they smoked it and laid it by. They took some rum out of a keg and poured it on the head of the grave, by way of giving it to their departed brother. Then they all drank. They repeated this until the spirit began to operate, and their hearts began to soften. They all fell to crying and making woeful noise for a while, until they thought wisely that they could not bring him back, and that an application to the keg was the best way to drown sorrow and wash away grief. The motion was soon executed, and all began to be merry as a party could be. They continued until near night. When they were more than half drunk, the men began to approach the women and chat freely. At length they began to lean on each other, kiss and act very amorous. In their way, the women made this visit to the dead a very pleasant one.

The next morning we proceeded up the Fox River, which was very serpentine. We came to a shallow lake where we could not see water except in the canoe track. The wild rice was so thick that the Indians could hardly get one of their small canoes into the rice to

Gathering wild rice, by Seth Eastman

gather it. Vast numbers of wild ducks fatten there on the wild rice every fall. When they rise, they make a noise like thunder. We killed as many as we chose, fat and good. The canoe track was so narrow that it took most of the next day to proceed about three miles with our large canoes. The water was too deep and the bottom was too soft for wading. Just at night we reached warm ground, and we feasted well after the fatigues of the day.

The next day we proceeded up the river, which is slack water but very serpentine. It is so winding that we had to paddle three miles to advance one. The banks are level with the water, and the meadows on each side are clothed with a good sort of grass. Back from the river the lands are as fine as can be imagined, with good but scattered timber. It is proverbial that the fires which run over these prairies destroy the small trees and stop the spread of the woods.

That night we reached the carrying place [the site of Portage, Wisconsin] and for two days of hard labor, we carried our canoes and goods over to the bank of the River Wisconsin. There we gummed our canoes fit to descend the river, and about midday we embarked. The River Wisconsin is a gentle, gliding stream. As we descended it, we saw many rattlesnakes swimming across, and we killed them.

The next day we arrived at a village of Saukies [Sauks] where we tarried for two days [the site of Prairie du Sac, Wisconsin]. The Sauks are of a good size, and less inclined to tricks and bad manners than their neighbors. They will take goods from traders on credit in the fall, and in the winter they will pay their debts. They are well disposed for "civilized" Indians. (Indians in general have been made worse by civilization.)

Their lodges are built with planks they hew out of wood for uprights. The tops are arched over with strong saplings and covered with tiles of bark. Some lodges are 60 feet long and contain several families. On each side of their lodges they raise a platform about two feet high and five feet wide, on which they sit and sleep.

In the fall the Sauks leave their village and go into the woods to hunt rabbits, bears and deer. They return in the spring before planting time. The women raise great crops of corn, beans, pumpkins

211

Winnebago medicine lodge, by Seth Eastman

and potatoes. Their amusements are singing, dancing, smoking, matches, gaming, feasting, drinking and hunting, and they are famous in magic. They are not very jealous of their women. The men often join in war parties with other nations, and go against Indians on the Missouri and farther west. Sometimes they go near Santa Fe in New Mexico, and bring back Spanish horses. I have seen many horses.

At night, when these people are seated around their fires, the elders tell of what they have seen and heard. The family listens. If there is a young girl in the lodge that any man of a different lodge has a liking for, he sits among them. He watches for an opportunity, and throws a small stick at her. If she looks up with a smile, it is a good omen. He repeats, and perhaps the girl returns the stick. The symptoms grow stronger. He takes notice of where she sits, for there she will sleep. When the family lies down to sleep, each person wraps up in a blanket. When all the family is quiet and perhaps asleep, he slips softly in and sits by her side. Presently he begins to lift her blanket in a soft manner. She may twitch it out of his hand with a sigh and a snore, but this is no killing matter. He sits awhile and makes a second attempt. She may hold the blanket down lightly. At length she turns over with a sigh and quits hold of the blanket. This method is practiced for a short time. Then the young man goes hunting. If he is lucky, he brings the lung and heart of an animal home to her family. This pleases them, and he begins to grow bold. After that, the girl will not refuse him. He will stay with the family for perhaps a year and hunt for the old father, but when the young couple begins to have children, they save what they can for their own use, and begin to live apart from her parents.

After I gave the Sauks credit until the next spring, I descended to a Fox village about 50 miles distant [near the site of Wauzeka, Wisconsin]. Here I met a different sort of people, who were bred at Detroit under the French government and clergy, until by being Christianized they grew so bad the French went to war against them, and killed great numbers of them. The rest fled to the Fox River where they made a stand, and pillaged traders going to the Mississippi. At length the French sent a strong party against them and beat them back to where they now live in sad circumstances.

213

As I approached this village, I saw a number of long, painted poles on which hung painted dogs, belts of wampum beads, silver bracelets and other articles. They told me they had just suffered a sweeping sickness that had killed a great number, and they were offering the articles as sacrifices to appease the spirit who was angry with them and had sent the sickness. I told them they were doing right, and should take care that they did not offend the spirit again.

We paddled down the Wisconsin River to its mouth, then paddled up the Mississippi River three miles where we came to the Plain of Dogs [Prairie du Chien], the great place of rendezvous for traders and Indians before they disperse to their wintering grounds. Here we met many Frenchmen giving credit to the Indians. All were to rendezvous there again in the spring. I stayed ten days, sending my nine clerks to different rivers that fall into the Mississippi.

When I had finished these matters in October, I set off with two other traders for St. Peters River [Minnesota River] which is 275 miles up the Mississippi. The season was favorable, and we went slowly to let the Nottawaseas [Sioux] pass onto the prairies. We did not want to be troubled with them asking for credit, for they are bad pay masters. In going up the Mississippi, we had plenty of fat ducks and geese, venison and bear's meat. We carried plenty of flour, tea, coffee, sugar, butter, spirits and wine. The banks of the river provided plenty of crab apples, which were very good when the frost touched them at the right time. We lived as well as our hearts could wish, and we fared well as voyageurs.

We entered the Minnesota River and proceeded up it as far as we thought best. About 14 miles up this river we saw the cabin where Jonathan Carver had passed a winter, marking the farthest extent of his travels. (I could have made Carver's whole tour in six weeks with one well-manned canoe.) We encamped on a high bank of the Minnesota River, so we would not be flooded in the spring when the ice broke up. We built comfortable cabins for the winter and got our goods under cover. In December some Indians on the plains sent young men to look for traders, and they found us. In January others began to approach us with dried and fresh meat, and skins of beaver, otter, deer, fox, wolf and racoon. We welcomed

214

them and did our business to advantage. Through the winter we proceeded eastward with ease and profit.

That spring as the ice broke up, the water rose 26 feet and made sad work with the river banks. When the water fell, we embarked and drifted down with the current to Prairie du Chien, where we saw people from every part of the Mississippi who had arrived before us. The French were very numerous. No fewer than 130 birchbark canoes had arrived from Mackinac, each carrying 6,000 to 8,000 pounds of goods. Boats came from the Illinois, and others came up the river 2,000 miles from New Orleans, each navigated by 36 men rowing as many oars. In a single boat they brought 60 barrels of wine, besides ham and cheese, to trade with the French and Indians. As for the natives, I have no true idea of their numbers. Their camps stretched for a mile and a half.

Here sports of all kinds were played. The French practiced billiards. The Indians played la crosse.

Yet I noticed that some of the Indians were uneasy. They told me there was a person at that place who had an evil spirit. He did things beyond their understanding. I went to see him, and I asked him many questions. I found him to be a Frenchman who lived among the nations on the Missouri. He was a master of magic, and he held such sway over those tribes that they agreed to most of his requests. They called him Manitou, which means "spirit" in their language. As this man was standing among some people, an Indian came up with a carefully wrought stone pipe in which he set great store. Manitou asked the Indian to let him look at it, and he offered to buy it, but the Indian would not part with it. Suddenly Manitou seemed to put the whole pipe in his mouth and swallow it. The poor Indian stood astonished—the pipe was three times larger than Manitou's mouth. Manitou told him not to trouble himself about it— the Indian would have his pipe again in two or three days, but it must first pass through his body. Two days later, Manitou offered the pipe to the Indian, who looked at it as if he could not bear to part with it, yet he would not put his hand upon it. Manitou kept the pipe for nothing.

215

We went to collecting furs and skins from the different tribes, with success. All my outfits did well. I had a great share for my part, as I had furnished by far the largest cargo on the river. After all business was done and people grew tired of sport, they began to leave Prairie du Chien. We too left with our peltries for Mackinac, and arrived there in July.

At Mackinac there was a great concourse of people from all quarters, some preparing to take their furs to Canada, others to Albany and New York, others to their intended wintering grounds. Others were trading with Indians from all parts for furs, skins, maple sugar, grease and tallow. Some were amusing themselves in good company, playing billiards, drinking fresh punch wine, feasting and dancing at night with respectable persons. The more vulgar were fighting each other.

I applied myself to fitting out a large and rich cargo of trade goods for the same parts of the country as the year before. But in August a trader arrived from Lake Superior with the bad news that the Sioux and the Chippewas were killing each other. This made it dangerous for traders to go into the country. The commander at Mackinac called a council of traders and asked that we use our ways and means to settle the dispute. We all contributed to make six large belts of wampum beads—three for the Sioux and three for the Chippewas—and the commander wrote speeches to both nations. I was bound for the center of the Sioux country, along the Minnesota River, so I was charged with the belts and a speech for the Sioux. Traders bound for Lake Superior were to carry the same to the Chippewas.

When I arrived at Minnesota River, I called eleven Sioux chiefs together, explained the speech and the intention of the belts, and convinced them to return with me to Mackinac to make peace. We embarked, and when we reached the mouth of the Minnesota River, we found traders there with a few Chippewa chiefs from the head of the Mississippi. I was much surprised to see them so bold among the Sioux, for the blood was scarcely cold; the wound was yet fresh. While we stayed there, a young Chippewa chief continually sang his death song, as if he despised the threats of the Sioux. When we

216

reached Prairie du Chien, we joined a vast number of Indians of all descriptions who were waiting for me to go to Mackinac. Many of these people had never before been out of their country except on war parties. The council at Mackinac excited the curiosity of every nation south of Lake of the Woods. Some chiefs traveled more than 2,000 miles to attend.

We left Prairie du Chien, and all of the many canoes made the best of their way up the Wisconsin River, crossed the portage as fast as they could, and descended Fox River to the bottom of Green Bay. There we joined other canoes bound for Mackinac.

The way was fair, and we proceeded together across Lake Michigan, every chief with his flock. After several days, we all appeared on the lake about five miles from Mackinac. We approached the fort in order, flying flags from the masts of our canoes. I hoisted the Union Jack when we were within a mile and a half. My canoes, being the largest in that part of the country, took the lead, and all the Indians followed close behind. The flag in the fort was hoisted, and the cannon of the garrison began to fire smartly. People of all sorts lined the shores and sent up such hollering that it set the tribes in the fleet to hooping. You could not hear a person speak. At length we landed, and the cannon ceased.

The people from Lake Superior had arrived before us. That day and the next the grand council was held before the English commander and a vast number of spectators. Articles of peace were concluded and great promises were made. The principal promise was that the Sioux should not cross east of the Mississippi, and the Chippewas should not cross to the west.

The next day a large, fat ox was killed and cooked by the soldiers. All the nations were invited to the feast. They dined together in harmony, and finished the day in drinking moderately, smoking together, singing and brightening the chain of friendship in a very decent way. After four days they all embarked for their own part of the country.

That fall I returned to Minnesota River and put my goods in the same cabin that I had wintered in the year before. Indians there told me of a large band of natives encamped up the river 200 miles to the west, who wanted to see a trader. The oldest of traders had never before attempted to visit them because of the rudeness of the people: a band of the Sioux nation called Yantonoes [Yanktons]. They had always lived on the prairies.

Their chief came to me and invited me to trade with them, and I immediately decided to put goods in a canoe and go up to them. We set off together, I by water in a canoe, the chief by land, cutting across the prairies. After nine days I knew we were close to their camp. It being wet and cold, we encamped and turned over my canoe, which made a grand shelter. That night it began to freeze, snow and blow hard. Early in the morning the wind lifted my canoe up into the air, and let it fall on the frozen flat of the river, breaking it in pieces. We were left in a sad situation, but about noon I saw a number of natives on the other side of the river—some on horseback, others on foot. They forded the river and offered to carry my goods to their camp. We loaded their horses and marched to their camp, where five natives met us: four carrying a finely painted beaver blanket, the other holding a pipe of peace. All were finely dressed, with feathers and painted hair. I could not understand one word they said, but from their actions I supposed it to be all friendship. After we smoked, they put on me a pair of fine moccasins, then they laid me on the blanket and carried me into a lodge among venerable old men. After smoking, an old man arose, solemnly laid his hands on my head, and groaned "Ay, ay, ay." He drew his right hand down on my arms, feigned a sort of cry as if shedding tears, and sat down. The others followed his example. At length an old man took food from one of the kettles—a sort of soup thick with pounded corn meal. He fed me three spoonfuls, then gave me a bark dish and a buffalo-horn spoon so I could feed myself. As soon as I finished my part of the feast, they carried me to another lodge where they had taken my people and goods. Six of their men carried spears to guard the goods from the crowd.

By the time I began to trade, the crowd had grown to at least 750 people. The chief who invited me had told me the trading was to begin at sundown, but he was absent, and they forced me to begin earlier. He also had told me they might take all that I had, because

218

Chief of the Yankton Sioux, by George Catlin

these people had never before seen a trader in their country, nor had they seen a bale of trade goods opened. I was in a bad situation, but at sundown the chief arrived, and seeing the large crowd, he posted six more guards and took charge himself. He kept up discipline as smart as I ever saw. One of the natives was especially daring, and continued to come close until a guard threw a spear at him. It drew a little blood, and he did not try again.

I continued my trade until near morning when they had no more furs to trade. They then prepared to leave because they had eaten all their food, and I had none to give them. By daylight, all had left except the chief. He kept near me to the last, to prevent any insult which might arise as they were going off. Late in the morning the chief left too.

I was now without any friends or assistance except my own men, and they could do little to acquire food, nor could they assist me in transporting my furs without a canoe. I decided to leave a boy to guard the furs until we could return with food. The poor fellow seemed willing to stay, but all we could give him were three handfuls of corn and two beaver skins with some meat on them. If we would be gone longer than we calculated, he could singe the hair off the skins, and roast them in the fire to stay alive.

We crossed the prairies to return to our cabin, where we found that the clerk had collected a little food. But hard weather then set in so that my men could not take food to the boy. Some days later they finally set off, and reached the boy 15 days after we had left him. He was well but feeble. They went to work and put the furs on a scaffold to be safe from wolves, then set off for home.

The day before they arrived at my cabin, they were overtaken on the prairie by a snow storm, so they could not see their way. There was no wood nearby, so they sat down on the prairie, wrapped their blankets about them, and let the snow cover them over. The next morning arrived clear, with the wind blowing out of the north-west, and freezing hard. They dug out of the snow, but they were wet, and although they had to walk only 10 more miles, their feet were badly frozen. The boy escaped as well as any of them—I believe

220

the best. I had a long job of healing them, but I did so without losing a limb.

In the spring I sent my people after the furs they had left on the scaffold the winter before. They took with them an Indian hunter who killed some buffalo. When they reached the furs, they cut down small saplings and made frames for two boats. They then sewed the buffalo skins together, stretched them across the frames, and rubbed them over with tallow. This made the boats tight enough to bring the furs down river to me.

The land along the Minnesota River is excellent, with some good timber. The woods and prairies are full of animals: turkeys, buffalo, deer, caribou, elk and moose. Racoons are very large. Snakes are small and not poisonous. Wolves are plentiful. They follow the buffalo and often kill the young and the old.

The Yankton Sioux are ferocious and rude, perhaps owing to their obscure life on the prairies. They seldom see their neighbors. They lead a wandering life on that extensive plain between the Missouri River and the Mississippi. They have many horses and dogs that carry their baggage when they move from place to place. They live in tents of leather spread across poles that meet at the top, in the shape of a bell. They build their fire in the middle, and at night they lie down around the tent with their feet to the fire. They use buffalo dung for fuel, because there is little or no wood upon the plains.

They run down the buffalo on their horses and kill as many as they please. To make their horses long-winded, they slit their noses up to the gristle of their heads, which makes them breath very freely.

They are always on the watch for their enemies, who are all around them. Their weapons include some fire arms, bows and arrows, and spears, which they always carry. When they are marching or riding, they put on shirts with sleeves that come down to the elbows, made of skins several layers thick to turn away arrows shot from a distance. When a number of them ride over the plains in advance of their band, they make a war-like appearance.

When a person among them dies in winter, they carry the body with them until they come to a spot of woods. There they put the

221

body on a scaffold until the frost is out of the ground and they can bury it. They believe in two spirits, one good and one bad.

The spring is now advancing fast. Chiefs are arriving to go with me to Mackinac.

DESPERATE ENTERPRISE

George Rogers Clark   1778–79

The American Revolution brought a wave of Indian attacks against settlers on the western frontier. At Detroit, British Governor Henry Hamilton urged Upper Country Indians to send war parties against the Kentucky frontier. He offered a bounty for American scalps, and he became known to Kentuckians as the "hair buyer." In 1778, a young Kentuckian named George Rogers Clark gained permission to raise troops to protect the frontier. His secret plan was to carry the fight to the British—to lead his small band of volunteers into enemy territory, and to seize British outposts.

I kept my destination a secret from my troops. I knew the impression it would make: to be taken almost a thousand miles from their country in order to attack a people who were five times their number and allied to merciless tribes of Indians. I knew my case was desperate, but the more I reflected on my weakness, the more I was pleased with the enterprise. I expected some of my troops to desert when they learned their destination. To prevent this, I encamped on a small island in the middle of the Falls of Ohio [at the site of Louisville, Kentucky] and kept strict guard on the boats. Even so, the men under Lieutenant Hutchings managed to escape.

On the 26th of June we set off from the falls, double-manning our oars, proceeding day and night down the Ohio River until the fourth day, when we ran into the mouth of the Tennessee River. We rested for the night, and in the morning we set off overland to the northwest for 50 miles, where we came to the level plains of an extensive country [now southern Illinois]. That country is more beautiful than any I could have imagined. Extending beyond eyesight are large prairies covered with buffalo and other game, varied by groves of trees that appear like islands in the sea. With a good eyeglass you can see all the buffalo for over half a million acres, so level is the country.

I knew my success depended on secrecy, so I was much afraid of being discovered. On these prairies we could have been seen for several miles. During our march my guide lost himself, and was unable to give a just account for himself. This put all my troops in the greatest confusion. I never in my life felt such a flow of rage: to be wandering about in a country where every nation of Indians could raise three or four times our number, and with certain loss of our enterprise if the enemy should be forewarned. I could not bear the thought of returning. Every idea of the sort put me in a passion. In a moment I decided to put the guide to death if he did not find his way by that evening. I told him of his doom, and the poor fellow, scared almost out of his wits, begged that I not be hard with him. He claimed that he could find the path. He soon took his course, and within two hours he knew where he was.

On the evening of the 4th of July, we got within three miles of the Town of the Kaskaskias, [near the mouth of the Kaskaskia River, Illinois], where we had to cross a river of the same name. We prepared ourselves for anything. After nightfall we marched to a farm on the same side of the river, where we took the family prisoners and found plenty of boats. In two hours we had crossed the river with the greatest silence. I then divided my little army into two divisions, ordered one to surround the town, and with the other I broke into the fort and captured the governor, Mr. Rochblave. In 15 minutes I had every street secured, and I sent runners through the town, ordering the people, on pain of death, to keep close to their houses. Before daylight I had the whole town disarmed.

Nothing could exceed the confusion of these people, who expected savage treatment from Americans. They gave up all for lost. Their lives were all they dared to beg for, which they did with great subserviance, offering to be slaves to save their families. When I told them it did not suit me to answer their pleas, they returned to their houses trembling as if led to the executioner. I would not have distressed so many people, except that it was necessary for my purpose. I realized I had to attach these people to me, for I was too weak to treat them in any other way.

I summoned all the important men of the town, who came cursing fortune that they had not been warned to defend themselves. I told them I was sorry they had so base an opinion of Americans and our cause. I told them they were a conquered people, and by fate of war they were at my mercy; but I added that our principle was to free those we conquered, not to enslave them. I told them that if I could be sure of their zeal and attachment to the American cause, they would immediately enjoy all the privileges of our government, and their property would be secured to them. I said we paid them this attention only to stop further shedding of innocent blood by the savages, who were under the influence of their governor.

No sooner did they hear this than joy sparkled in their eyes. They said they had been kept in the dark as to the dispute between America and Britain, but they were now convinced they should unite with the Americans. The priest, a Mr. Gibault, recently arrived from Canada, asked if I would give him liberty to perform his duties in his church. I told him that I had nothing to do with churches, except to defend them from insult. This seemed to complete their happiness.

In the meantime I prepared a detachment on horseback, under Captain Bowman, to descend on Cohos [Cahokia, in St. Clair County, Illinois]. The residents of Kaskaskia told me that I could take possession of Cahokia if just one of their townsmen carried the good news there. I did not altogether trust them, so I dispatched the captain with a number of the residents. They reached the middle of the town before they were discovered, and once there, a French gentleman

225

called aloud to the people to submit to their happier fate, which they did with little hesitation. A number of Indians in the town heard of the Big Knives [the Indian name for Americans] and immediately made their escape.

Post St. Vincent [now Vincennes, Indiana] was the next object in my view. By now that town had been forewarned of my actions, and I could by no means march against it; so I decided to try to win their affection. I pretended that I was about to send word to Falls of Ohio for more troops to join me, to attack Vincennes. Advocates at Kaskaskia immediately stepped forward on behalf of the residents of Vincennes. The priest, Mr. Gibault, offered to try to win that town for me. He said that, although he had nothing to do with temporal business, he would give them hints in a spiritual way that would be very helpful to my cause. In a few days the priest and several others set out with a proclamation I wrote. A few weeks later they returned with most agreeable news. I found myself in possession of the whole country.

Yet most of my men now favored returning to Virginia, as they were no longer engaged, yet found themselves surrounded by nations of savages whose minds had long been poisoned by the English. With great presents and promises, I managed to reenlist about 100 of them for eight months. Many of the French, fond of the service, also enlisted.

Domestic affairs in order, I now turned my attention to the Indian department. My sudden appearance in their country had bewildered them. They were generally at war against us, but they were also confused by the fondness that the French and the Spanish showed for us. They consulted with French traders, who told them to come to us and make peace. I quickly acquainted myself with the French and Spanish mode of dealing with the Indians, and decided to follow it. The Kaskaskias, Peorias and Michigameas immediately asked for peace. I sent word to the Kickapoos and Piankashaws at Vincennes to lay down the tomahawk, or to behave like men and to continue to fight for the English. I added that they would soon see their great English father, as they called him, thrown to the dogs to be eaten. (I used harsh language, knowing well that it was a mistake to think

226

that soft speeches are best for Indians.) I said that if they would give their hands to the Big Knives, they should give their hearts as well. After some counciling, they decided to take the Big Knives by the hand and make peace. They said Americans must be warriors to speak as we did. They said that they liked such people, and that the English were liars.

At Cahokia I delivered a speech to the Indians, part of which explained the war in the following manner: A great many years ago, our forefathers lived in England, but the king oppressed them so that they crossed the great waters to get out of his way. Not being satisfied with losing so many subjects, the king sent governors and soldiers after them, to make them obey his laws. He told his governors to treat them well, and to take but little from them until they grew populous, when they would be able to pay a great deal. By this good treatment we grew to be a great people, and we quickly flourished. The king then wrote to his governors and officers that we had gotten rich and numerous enough. It was time to make us pay tribute. He wrote that he did not care how much the governors took, just so they left us enough to eat. He sent a great many soldiers. Once they had made us do as they pleased, they planned to make the Indians pay likewise. To keep the Indians from learning about this from the Big Knives, the king ordered his governors to make the Indians and the Big Knives quarrel with one another. We paid their taxes for many years. At last the taxes were so hard that if we killed a deer, they would take the skin and leave us only the meat. Then they would make us buy blankets with our corn, so they could feed their soldiers. By such abuse we became poor and were forced to go naked. At last we complained. This angered the king, and he made his soldiers kill some of our people and burn some of our villages. Our old men then held a great council, made the tomahawk very sharp, put it into the hands of our young men, and told us to be strong and to strike the English, as long as we could find one on this land. The young men immediately struck and killed a great many of the English. The French king heard of this and sent word to us, telling us that we should be strong and fight the English, and that if we wanted help or tomahawks, he would send them.

227

This speech had a greater effect on the Indians than I could have imagined, and did more service than a whole regiment of men could have done. We were astonished to see the amazing number of savages who came to Cahokia to make peace with the Big Knives. Many of them came from 500 miles distant: Chippewas, Ottawas, Potawatomies, Missisaugas, Winnebagoes, Sauks, Foxes, Osages, Tamaroas, Miamis and a number of other nations living east of the Mississippi. Many of them had been at war against us.

When all these Indians arrived at Cahokia, I must confess that I was worried among so many devils, and justly so. On the second or third night a band of Winnebagoes tried to force by the guards and carry me off. Happily they were detected, and taken prisoners by the alacrity of the sergeant. The whole town took alarm and was quickly under arms, thus convincing the savages that the French residents were in our interest. I decided to take harsh action, regardless of the consequences. I ordered the French militia to put all the chiefs in irons. This created great confusion among the rest of the savages, who were at a loss what to do, because I had strong guards in every quarter of the town. The imprisoned chiefs asked to speak with me, but I refused. I told all of them that I believed they were a set of villains, and I welcomed them to continue in the English cause. I told them I was a man and a warrior. I did not care who was my friend or foe. I had no more to say to them. My action alarmed the whole town, but I knew it would gain us no more enemies than we already had, and it might have a lasting effect on the Indian nations. I showed my disregard for the Indians by staying in my lodging 100 yards outside the fort, apparently unguarded. (In truth, 50 armed men were hiding in my parlor.) During the night a great council was held among the Indians. To show more disregard for them I invited gentlemen and ladies to my house to dance nearly the whole night through.

In the morning I summoned the nations to a grand council, and I released the chiefs so I might speak to them in front of all. I showed them a bloody belt of beads, and I told the guilty Winnebago chief that I knew his nation favored the English. I said that if they thought it right, I did not blame them for it. I exhorted them to behave like

Winnebago brave, by George Catlin

men, and to support their cause. I said I knew the English were weak and wanted help, and I scorned taking advantage of the English by persuading their friends to desert them. I said most people would put them to death for their behavior, but it was beneath the character of Americans to take such revenge. I told them they were at liberty to leave, and I would have them escorted safely out of the village if they agreed not to do mischief for three days. After that time they could choose to return to fight me, or they could find Americans enough to fight by going elsewhere. I offered them the war belt, and I said we would soon see which of us would make it more bloody.

The other nations rose and excused their actions with beautiful and noble sentiments. They said they had been urged to war by the English, who had given them the wrong opinion of Americans. They said they now believed us to be men and warriors, and they wished to take us by the hand as brothers. They asked me to favor the guilty Winnebagoes, which I refused to do.

A speaker for the Winnebagoes then rose and made a most lamentable speech, begging for mercy for their wives and children, just as I had hoped he would. I suggested the Winnebagoes go to their English father, who had promised he would help them. I said they should blame no one but themselves when their nation and the English were thrown to the dogs. After their eloquence failed, the Winnebagoes presented two young men for me to put to death, hoping this would pacify me. The two young men presented themselves for death, walking to the middle of the floor, sitting down next to each other, and covering their heads with their blankets to receive the blow from the tomahawk. This act quickly won my favor, and for a few moments I was so agitated that I would have killed the first man who offered to hurt them. I granted mercy, and a treaty was soon completed.

Our influence now began to spread among all the nations, even to the border of the lakes. I sent my agents into every quarter. Don Leybrau, Spanish governor at St. Louis, soon showed his support for the American cause.

By this time the English at Detroit, seeing that they were losing their influence among the savages, sent their own agents out as far

230

as they dared venture. They redoubled their presents and insinuations. We discovered a young man at Cahokia sending intelligence to Governor Hamilton at Detroit. We expected that Hamilton would attack Kaskaskia, our strongest garrison and our headquarters; but instead he descended the Wabash River with 800 men—French, Indians, and British regulars—and easily recaptured Vincennes on December 17th.

Hard weather was now setting in, and I was at a loss to know what to do. I was ready to evacuate Cahokia in case of a siege. But in the height of our anxiety, on the 29th of January, a Spanish merchant arrived from Vincennes and told me all that I wished to know about the enemy. He said Hamilton's force had included about 800 men when he captured Vincennes; but finding the winter too far advanced to move against Kaskaskia, he had sent nearly all of his Indians off in war parties. He had told them to return as soon as the weather permitted, to complete the attack on us. He also had sent word to the southern Indians, and he expected 500 to join him soon.

I now saw that our best chance for keeping the country was to take advantage of Hamilton's present weakness. I considered the harsh weather and the bad trails to be to our advantage, as the enemy would now be off guard. I called my officers and told them I thought we could tip the scale in our favor. Every one of them was eager for it. We began to act as though we were sure of defeating Hamilton, and in a day or two the whole country believed us. Many volunteers turned out. The ladies showed spirited interest in the expedition, which had great effect on the young men.

On the 5th of February we set out on a forlorn hope indeed. Our whole party consisted of little more than 200 men. I cannot explain it, yet I had inward assurance of success. We now faced a journey 240 miles in length, through, I suppose, one of the most beautiful countries in the world. But at this season the march was exceedingly bad, with many parts under cold, flowing water. My greatest care was to divert the men and to keep up their spirits.

We met the first great obstacle on February 13th, arriving at the two little Wabashes. Normally three miles apart, they now made but one river, five miles wide, with water flowing three or four feet deep.

231

George Rogers Clark raids Vincennes, by George Parrish, Jr.

This would have stopped any group of men not in the same temper as we. In three days we contrived to cross by building a large canoe which ferried us across the two channels. The rest of the way we waded through the frigid water. It rained for nearly a third of our march, but we never halted for it. On the evening of the 17th we reached the lowlands of the River Umbara [Embarass River], nine miles below Vincennes. Most of it was at least three feet under water. I will not give details of our suffering during the four days spent in crossing those waters. It would be too incredible for any person to believe.

To our inexpressible joy, on the 23rd we safely reached solid ground at a grove of trees which offered a full view of the desired fort. Lying in this grove to dry our clothes in the sun, we soon took a prisoner who was friendly to our cause, from whom we learned all we needed to know.

A thousand ideas flushed across my mind at this moment. I learned that Governor Hamilton could defend himself for a considerable time within the fort, but he was too weak to turn out against us. I knew if the siege continued long, a superior force would come against us, as there was a party of English not far above us on the river. I decided to appear as daring as possible, so the enemy might think by our actions that we were numerous. I immediately wrote to the residents in general, informing them of where I was and what I intended to do, and asking the friends of the United States to keep close to their houses. I told those in the British interest to go to the fort and to fight for their king. I sent the compliments of several officers who were not even with me to several gentlemen in the town.

Between the town and the wood that covered us was an open field. We started to march against the fort before dark, but we placed our lines to take advantage of the land, so that only our flags could be seen. We had flags enough for 1,000 men; and the residents of the town, who could count only our colors, judged our numbers accordingly. I detached a party to attack the fort, and with the main body I took possession of the strongest positions in the town. Firing soon began very warmly from both sides. A number of Indians in the English cause made their escape out of town, while about 100

233

Kickapoos and Piankashaws immediately took up arms in our favor, and marched to attack the fort. I thanked the chief, but warned him of the danger of our people mingling in the dark, so he ordered his men to their quarters until daylight. The artillery from the fort played briskly, but did no damage. We surrounded the fort and fired from behind houses, yards and ditches, from a distance of 80 to 100 yards. Within a few hours I began to believe that my prize was assured. I now felt certain of taking every one of the enemy who had incited the Indians to war against us. All my past sufferings vanished. Never was a man happier. My troops needed no encouragement to inflame their spirits. They knew the person they were attacking, and they remembered their massacred friends. Every place of cover near the fort was crowded with them, and heavy firing continued into the night.

The next morning I ordered our firing stopped, and sent a note to Mr. Hamilton, recommending that he surrender. He answered that his garrison was not inclined to be awed into any act unbecoming British soldiers.

During the pause the Kickapoos discovered a band of warriors who were returning from Kentucky with two American prisoners. The Kickapoos met them at the town commons. The warriors believed the Kickapoos had been sent to honor them by conducting them into the fort. I was greatly pleased to see each party whooping, hollering and striking their breasts as they met in the open field, trying to outdo each other with the greatest signs of joy. Those poor devils did not learn their mistake until the Kickapoos suddenly fell upon them. Six were taken prisoner, two were scalped, and the rest were so wounded that only one lived. I now had a chance to impress the Indians inside the fort that Governor Hamilton could not protect them as he had told them he could. I ordered that the Indian prisoners be tomahawked in front of the fort. This had the effect I expected. Indians inside the fort scolded the English for not trying to save their friends, calling the English liars and cowards.

A remarkable thing then happened. An old French gentleman, a lieutenant of my volunteers from Cahokia, had but one son. This son happened to be leading the captured Indians. He was made a prisoner, and the question was asked whether the white man should be saved. I ordered him put to death. Not recognizing his son who was painted like an Indian, the father drew his sword and stood by him, to run him through if he should stir. The son, seeing the tomahawk raised for its fatal stroke, raised his eyes to heaven and cried, "Oh, save me!" The father recognized his son's voice, and the two were shaken to encounter each other at such a critical moment. I had so little mercy for the murderer, and so great a chance to set an example, that I walked away. But after hearing the warmest pleas from the father, who had served us so well, I granted the son's life.

Governor Hamilton soon afterward met with me and agreed to my articles of surrender. At the surrender I took almost as many prisoners as I had men, so I needed to get rid of many of them. I treated most of them well, to promote my interests, then I freed them after they took an oath of neutrality. They went off huzzaing for the Congress. I later learned that they convinced some of their friends at Detroit in favor of America. I then sent Governor Hamilton and his officers to the Falls of Ohio, as prisoners.

Having settled matters a little, the Indian department came next. I knew that Governor Hamilton had tried to convince the Indians that we Americans intended at last to take all their lands from them; that if we would win the war, we would show no mercy for them. I learned of the arguments he used, then I called together the neighboring nations: Piankashaws, Kickapoos and others. I made a long speech to them in the Indian manner, praising them to the skies for their manly courage and fidelity. I told them that I had no design on their lands; that I believed we were even then on their land, even where the fort stood; that any man who tried to take their lands by violence must first strike the tomahawk in my head; that I was in their country only during the war to keep a fort and to drive off the English, who plotted against all people; and that after the war I would go off to some other place.

Soon a treaty was concluded, which satisfied the Indians as well as the Americans.

235

LAST
SUN

Chief Black Hawk 1832

*At age 64, a Sauk chief named Black Hawk led a large
band of Sauk and Fox Indians against American settlers who had encroached on tribal lands in Illinois.
Within a few months, Black Hawk's people were hunted
down and massacred by American soldiers. As Black
Hawk was delivered into captivity, he made the following speech.*

My warriors fell around me. I saw my evil day
at hand. The sun rose clear on us in the
morning; at night it sank in a dark cloud and
looked like a ball of fire. This was the last sun that shone on Black
Hawk. He is now a prisoner to the white man. But he can stand the
torture. He is not afraid of death. He is no coward. Black Hawk is
an Indian. He has done nothing of which an Indian need be ashamed.
He has fought the battles of his country against the white man, who
came year after year to cheat Black Hawk's people and to take away
their lands. Black Hawk is satisfied. He will go to the world of spirits
contented. He has done his duty. His father will meet him and reward
him.

You know the cause of our making war. It is known to all white
men. They ought to be ashamed of it. White men despise Indians
and drive them from their homes. White men do not scalp the head,

236

but they do worse—they poison the heart. It is not pure with them. Black Hawk's countrymen will not be scalped, but in a few years they will become like the white man, so they cannot be hurt.

Farewell to my nation. Farewell to Black Hawk.

SOURCES

A COUNTRY FULL OF DARKNESS
>William R. Smith, ed. *The History of Wisconsin.* Madison, 1854. Vol. 3. 17–19.

CAESARS IN THE WILDERNESS; FAMINE; NATION OF THE BUFFALO
>Pierre E. Radisson. *Voyages of Peter Esprit Radisson.* Boston. 1885. 173–241.

THIS ADORED STATION
>Reuben G. Thwaites, ed. *Jesuit Relations and Allied Documents.* Cleveland. 1899. Vol. 48. 115–143.

SPIRITS
>Ibid. Vol. 50. 285–295.

I AM THE DAWN
>Emma Blair, ed. *Indian Tribes of the Upper Mississippi Valley.* Cleveland. 1910. Vol. 1. 308–347.

PARADISE
>Reuben G. Thwaites, ed. *Jesuit Relations and Allied Documents.* Cleveland. 1898. Vol. 55. 190–199. Vol. 56. 121–133.

GREAT RIVER
>*Louisiana Historical Collections.* New York. 1850. Vol. 2. 279–297.

FATAL WINTER
>John G. Shea, ed. *Discovery and Exploration of the Mississippi Valley.* New York. 1853. 53–66.

FRESHWATER SEAS; PRAIRIE; CAPTURED BY THE SIOUX
>Father Louis Hennepin. *Description of Louisiana.* New York. 1880. 69–258.

239

TOILSOME JOURNEY; WE ARE ALL SAVAGES
>Melville B. Anderson, ed. *Relation of the Discoveries and Voyages of Cavalier de la Salle from 1679 to 1681.* Chicago. 1901. 133–239.

ARM OF IRON
>*Louisiana Historical Collections.* New York. 1846. Vol. 1. 52–78.

PLENTITUDE
>Ibid. Vol. 1. 85–194.

MISSION TO THE ILLINOIS
>William I. Kip, ed. *The Early Jesuit Missions in North America.* New York. 1846. 30–43.

MOST BEAUTIFUL COUNTRY
>Father Antoine Silvy. *Letters from North America.* Translated by Ivy A. Dickson. Mika Publishing Co. Belleville, Ontario. 1980. 166–189.

CADILLAC'S MIRACLE
>*Michigan Pioneer and Historical Collections.* Lansing. 1904. Vol. 33. 133–151.

WAR WITHOUT MERCY
>Ibid. Vol. 33. 498–506.

THE FOX IS IMMORTAL
>*Collections of the State Historical Society of Wisconsin.* Madison. 1902. Vol. 16. 293–295.

BETWEEN TWO FIRES
>Ibid. 1906. Vol. 17. 36–62.

TO DESTROY A NATION
>Ibid. Vol. 17. 182–190.

A STORM ABOUT TO BURST
>Ibid. 1908. Vol. 18. 104–116.

HALF-BREED WARRIOR
Ibid. 1857. Vol. 3. 198–231.

A STRANGER TO THE TRADE; ATTACK ON MACKINAC;
FRIEND AND BROTHER
Alexander Henry. *Travels and Adventures in
Canada and the Indian Territories.* Boston. 1901.

PONTIAC'S REBELLION
Michigan Pioneer and Historical Collections.
Lansing. 1885. Vol. 8.

UNKNOWN DOMINION
Jonathan Carver. *Three Years Travels Through the
Interior Parts of North America.* Boston. 1802. 6–
83.

FUR TRADER
*Collections of the State Historical Society of
Wisconsin.* Madison. 1908. Vol. 18. 314–380.

DESPERATE ENTERPRISE
George Rogers Clark. *Col. George Rogers Clark's
Sketch of His Campaign in the Illinois in 1778-9.*
Cincinnati. 1869.

LAST SUN
Frank E. Stevens. *The Blackhawk War.* Chicago.
1903. 239.

ART

Illustrations in *Up Country* were selected for their authenticity. They include reproductions of art by some of America's great frontier artists. Foremost among the artists is George Catlin. In 1830, at age 34, Catlin seized upon "an enterprise of art on which to devote a whole lifetime of enthusiasm." He resolved to "rescue from oblivion the looks and customs of the vanishing races of natives in North America." Over the next decade, Catlin carried his paints and canvasses across the American frontier, capturing in superb detail the traditional dress and customs of many threatened Indian cultures.

Seth Eastman was an artist and a soldier. In the 1840's he commanded at Fort Snelling, where the Minnesota River joins the Mississippi. There he painted Sioux and Winnebago Indians against a backdrop of wilderness landscapes.

Frederic Remington is famous for his paintings and drawings of the Far West. But Remington also travelled to Canada twice, and in the 1890's he illustrated magazine stories about French voyageurs and fur traders.

Robert Thom is a contemporary artist. In the 1960's he was commissioned by Michigan Bell Telephone Company and by Illinois Bell Telephone Company to paint historic scenes for each of the states. His paintings were carefully researched, and historically accurate.

Use of the art in *Up Country* was generously permitted by the parties credited on the copyright page.